You

You

Orest Bedrij

AMITY HOUSE
Warwick, New York

3/96

Copyright 1988 by Orest Bedrij

Published by Amity House Inc.
16 High Street
Warwick, N.Y. 10990

Printed and bound in the United States of America

Library of Congress Catalog Card Number
88-72119

ISBN: 0-916349-78-0

Bookstore

This book is dedicated to you, my joy;
You—the Absolute Love, the Light of the world!
You, who smiles forth from every face!
You, in your own splendor of glory!

CONTENTS

v

ACKNOWLEDGEMENTS

I am deeply grateful to the hundreds of men and women who helped me with this project, not to mention the many who influenced my thinking long before the book was conceived.

In particular, I give grateful thanks, love, and credit to the propeller and light of my life, Melchizedek.

I am greatly indebted to my dearest friend and brother, Jesus the Christ, for his love, guidance, and encouragement. Furthermore, a special thank you and love to him for his willingness to descend from such great celestial heights, some two thousand years ago, to bring us the light, the way, and the truth of the Father.

Sincerest thanks, love, and blessings to my beautiful wife, Oksana, for her unending love, support, understanding, and for joining me in this task as an intimate advisor and companion.

A special thank you, love, and blessings to my lovely children, Adrian, Chrystyna, Marta, Orest, and Roksana, for their constant love, feedback, hugs, and frequent helpful discussions.

Sincerest thanks, love, and heartful appreciation to Richard Payne for his priceless suggestions and editing, which made this work possible.

Most of all, grateful acknowledgement and profound thanks to: Gautama the Buddha, Vyasa, Albert Einstein, Erwin Schroedinger, David

Bohm, Pierre Teilhard de Chardin, Meher Baba, Werner Heisenberg, Evelyn Underhill, Mahatma Gandhi, Max Planck, Aldous Huxley, Isaac Newton, James Clerk Maxwell, Mother Teresa, and thousands of others whose literary works are the shoulders I have stood on to produce this book.

Also, sincerest thanks and appreciation to: Lisbeth Aaggard, Christopher L. Arpa, Carol Cottrell, Jane De Forest, Billings Fuess, Norman Gorbaty, Samuel B. Lee, Mary Manilla, Bernice Neben, Alan Rogers, Martha Walsh, and Peter Wragg for their valuable reviewing efforts and suggestions.

Grateful acknowledgement is made to the following for their kind permission to use copyrighted material from the sources indicated below:

Aurora Press, P.O. Box 573, Santa Fe, NM 87501,
Tilling the Soul, Wingate, 1984.

Associated Book Publishers Ltd. (Ark Paperbacks), London, England, *Wholeness and The Implicate Order,* David Bohm, 1983.

The Catholic Press, Washington, D.C., *The New American Bible,* Confraternity of Christian Doctrine, 1970.

Frederick Fell Publishers, Inc., Glendale, CA, *The Greatest Salesman in the World,* Og Mandino, 1973.

The Theosophical Publishing House, Quest Books, Wheaton, IL, *The Essential Unity of All,* Das Bhagavan, 1973.

PREFACE

When Manuel Lisa, an Indian trader, accompanied by John Colter, a trapper and explorer (said to be the first white man to see the Yellowstone geysers), reported the spectacular thermal phenomena of thousands of mud volcanoes and erupting hot springs, no one would believe the story.

It was after others *saw* and *verified* the broad volcanic plateau with its 10,000 geysers, lakes, and rivers, mammoth hot springs, majestic waterfalls, eroded lava flows, black obsidian (volcanic glass) mountains, buffalo, elk, deer, moose, bear, and of course, Old Faithful, that the Yellowstone story became believable.

Like the Yellowstone explorers, other men and women throughout the short history of our planet have also given spectacular accounts of who we are. Some of these "reporters" were elevated to gods. Others were persecuted and even killed for relating "ridiculous" stories about their understanding of nature and of our position in nature.

The purpose of this book is to *wed* the texts of sacred tradition and the texts of physics. It is to *wed* the ideas of scholars, thinkers, and "gods" of the sacred traditions and the ideas of physical scientists, mathematicians, and cosmologists of the secular and scientific traditions. The object is to show that ALL are corroborating the same truth of who we are, and the future of our human civilization.

Forgive my extensive use of quotations. I believe the subject matter to be critical to our life and future happiness. It was necessary to bring into focus this voluminous body of material, with its exhaustive enumerations and references, along with the very words of those who authored the insights.

A world view based on information of this nature, if it is to become an important part of our lives, must be scientifically verifiable. Hence, I have used the "observers" (physical and spiritual physicians, sociologists, psychologists, biologists, literary theorists, historians of art and culture, physicists and mathematicians) from many countries and different centuries who have cleared their intellect sufficiently to elucidate the elements of our inquiry.

Although there are many different quotations from the Bible and other religious references, the purpose of this writing is not to support any individual religious dogma or denomination, but to precipitate scientific inquiry into the subject of Who We Are.

In the beginning, whether it was fixing the calendar of seasons or studying celestial omens, plotting the course of heavenly bodies, measuring the Nile water levels, determining the optimum planting and harvesting time or cataloging biological life, in most cases this work was initiated by priests and other high officials of the temple.

As a particular inquiry acquired scientific depth and validity, some beliefs became *verifiable* facts. The subject matter left the temples of faith and speculation and became living truths in homes, schools, and communities. This was the case with astronomy, education, agriculture, biology, and so forth.

Today, we are on a new plateau of history. The tools of science and mathematics can now be the instruments for transforming yet another speculation into fact; where we can start worshiping the truth and the light, and not just the messenger of the truth—the lamp, which brings the light. Today, we are at a point in time where we no longer have to fight religious wars about who said it, but rather *understand* what is being said. Today, we are about to undergo revisions of the concepts of time, space, matter, and energy more drastic than those engendered by relativity and quantum physics.

Throughout Part I of this book I will be focusing on insight into the various aspects of our Being. In Part II I will be focusing on scientific verification, testing, and validation through physics and mathematics. To make the facts more enjoyable and more digestible, I have leaned heavily on information already known and assimilated by you, the reader.

Why? Using the words of Stephen Hawking, widely regarded as the most brilliant theoretical physicist since Einstein, in his beautiful *A Brief History of Time:*

> so that we shall all, philosophers, scientists, and just ordinary people, be able to take a part in the discussion of the question of why it is that we and the universe exist. If we find the answer to that, it would be the ultimate triumph of human reason—for then we would know the mind of God.

Now let us go beyond relativity and quantum theory. Let us enjoy an orchestra whose musicians include Jesus the Christ, Gautama the Buddha, Albert Einstein, Werner Heisenberg, Mother Teresa, Erwin Schroedinger, David Bohm, Max Planck, John of the Cross, Aldous Huxley, George Santayana, William James, Alfred Whitehead, Pierre Teilhard de Chardin, Teresa of Avila, Meister Eckhart, Meher Baba, Mahatma Gandhi, Rupert Sheldrake, John Archibald Wheeler, Arthur Eddington, et al. They will be performing the greatest concerto of all.

Its theme is You.

INTRODUCTION

Throughout the brief history of mankind, many great thinkers, scholars, and scientists had *parallel* insights into who we are and from where we have come. More recently, with the tools of modern physics, mathematics, and high-speed computers, many more people are beginning to see into the inner core—the fundamental essence of our Being.

The facts are inescapable. The physical proof is unassailable. Time, space, gravity, matter, energy, all of nature's activities, and everyone you know and don't yet know are *interconnected*. Physical quantities, atoms, molecules, galaxies, you, your family, and your associates are all *the same one essence—the same one thing* in different states and forms.

Big breakthroughs are coming. The nature of our experience of the world is about to change. A new synthesis, which should lead to a more meaningful unity in our experience, may be based on knowledge at the leading edge of the individual sciences. With the insight of the greatest minds of history and the power of physics and mathematics, a breathtaking opportunity is ours. It is to awaken from the land of shadows—to try to remember Who We Are—to be That Which We Are.

What is left is to look to the sky, if we want to climb to the top of the tree of life. If we want cosmic union with light, love and human intimacy surpassing all understanding, then let us walk together. Let us advance in our knowledge.

Here is the opportunity to gasp and be in awe. To realize, using the tools of modern science and history, that *there is no one else within your robe but the Creator himself or herself!* You are the Light of the world! You are looking forth from every face—you, in your own splendor of glory. Salutation unto You!

Partake more fully in this ecstatic multi-dimensional Journey of Light. It was prepared for you before the creation of our spacetime for your enjoyment now.

Rejoice. Rejoice. Rejoice. Build upon what thus far has been achieved. Bring light where there is darkness. Let the fire of love, happiness, and peace burn! *For this you were born.*

I love you!

Orest

You

PART I

INSIGHTS:
A GREAT VISION
OF YOU

FROM
DARKNESS
TO LIGHT

From ignorance we come to belief;
Through belief we achieve knowledge;
And with knowledge we reach understanding.
Understanding in action is wisdom;
Wisdom in action is love;
And love in action is Christ manifest.

WHO
AM
I?

How would you like, for excitement and amusement, to clothe yourself in a robe of time, space, and matter and live as a salty ocean, a tall
sequoia tree, a beautiful woman, or a handsome man? How many
billions of years will it take you, in that new form, to perceive who you
are again?

What should the goal of our human aspiration be?

How can you prevent war, hunger, and mega-deficits? How can you
face millions of other human challenges?

Who am I? What am I? Why am I? What kind of world is this?

How do you upgrade the sacrament of sexual union to a more
elevated bliss?

What is the nature of reality and the unified theory of physics?

What do all of the above statements have in common? Together let us
explore.

Recently, Giscard d'Estaing, the former President of France, observed:

The world is unhappy. It is unhappy because it doesn't know
where it is going and because it senses that if it knew, it would
discover that it was heading for disaster.[1]

In *Civilization,* Kenneth Clark shares his personal view of where we are going:

> I have followed the ups and downs of civilization historically, trying to discover results as well as causes; well, obviously I can't do that any longer. We have no idea where we are going, and sweeping, confident articles on the future seem to me, intellectually, the most disreputable of all forms of public utterance. The scientists who are best qualified to talk have kept their mouths shut.[2]

What then, are the answers in this landscape of time, space, and matter? The questions have been asked by the scientist and layman, time and time again, in every country on our planet. For most, the problems remained unsolved; yet, here and there, at various times in history, a few did break through the haze. They understood who they were. They penetrated the secrets of how to prevent crime and sickness, how to deal with millions of other human challenges. They solved the problems of building peace, love, and harmony.

The following anonymous story from the Second World War illustrates how suffering can be transformed into healing harmony:

> During the war I was a witness to men and women being beaten to a bloody pulp, ears cut off, eyes taken out, and endless numbers of horrible deaths. I saw hundreds of people murdered and sprayed with sulphuric acid. I lived through the bombs falling and the people being exploded apart, with concentration camps and bed bugs, living with TB and the eating of worm-filled cabbage in order to stay alive. This was the same war that saw my wife deported to Siberia's Gulag Archipelago and then to Dachau.
>
> First, there was only horror and revulsion within me. But later as I researched the atrocities of those and other death factories, a question began rising up in my consciousness: How could people do this to others? How is this possible?
>
> Finally I began to cry as the pain of the whole reality started to permeate my being. Slowly, from the gift of tears came a growing compassion. And from the compassion came a desire to do something that would change things. And I was

moved to discover who we are. And I discovered that I am You. And in this discovery came the action. I was to *live* for You, in You, and with You.

Although the truth has always been there, because of limited communication and awareness, it is only recently that most people on our planet have become ready to understand the essential message of You and who You are.

Imagine for a moment an orchestra playing your favorite concerto. Ah! Feel the music. Instead of letting the musicians perform your beautiful piece together, isolate each player in a soundproof booth. Being skilled musicians, they will still execute the piece in harmony. Now, imagine that you have a remote control switch and can choose to tune in on each player individually. Because you know the piece, you will be able to relate each individual part to the whole concerto.

Visualize a situation in which several people, none of whom is familiar with your favorite concerto, are assigned to listen to only the tuba, the cymbals, the kettle drums, or the viola. Will they hear what you heard? How can they if they do not know the piece?

Our challenge resembles those who could not comprehend the Great Concerto. We keep fighting each other on personal, local, national, and international levels, believing that the instrument we perceive represents the total grandeur of the Great Concerto, that it is unique, that it belongs to us alone, that it gives us a monopoly. Sometimes, in the name of our convictions, we are even able to muster up enough self-justification and daring to hurt our fellow man.

David Bohm, one of the world's most eminent physicists, is a theorist of the non-fragmentary world view. He was profoundly affected by his close contact with Albert Einstein and Krishna Murti. He says:

One may suggest here that we are in a position which is in certain ways similar to where Galileo stood when he began his inquiries. A great deal of work has been done showing the inadequacy of old ideas, which merely permits a range of new facts to be *fitted mathematically* [comparable to what was done by Copernicus, Kepler, and others], *but we have not yet freed ourselves thoroughly from the older order of thinking,* using language and observation. We *have*

6

thus yet to perceive a new order. As with Galileo, this must involve seeing new differences so that much of what has been thought to be basic in the old ideas will be perceived to be more or less correct, but not of primary relevance [as happened, for example, with some of the key ideas of Aristotle]. When we see new basic differences, then [as happened with Newton] we will be able to perceive a new universal ratio or reason relating and unifying all the differences. This may ultimately carry us far beyond quantum theory and relativity as Newton's ideas went beyond those of Copernicus.[3]

Albert Einstein's intuitive and mathematical abilities contributed to the special and general relativity theory, the Brownian movement theory, and the quantum photoelectric effect. He had an authentic and deep grasp of the sublime mystery of the Great Concerto. He stated:

The highest principle for our aspirations and judgments is given to us in the Jewish-Christian religious tradition. It is a very high goal which, with our weak powers, we can reach only very inadequately, but which gives a sure foundation to our aspirations and valuations. If one were to take that goal out of its religious form and look merely at its human side, one might state it perhaps thus: *free and responsible development of the individual, so that he may place his powers freely and gladly in the service of mankind.*[4]

Jesus, whose riveting insights, life, and very name evoke love in my heart, was such a servant. He taught, using the instrument appropriate to his time, a message of the intimate relationship between truth, knowledge, and freedom. "Know the truth, and the truth will set you free" (John 8:32).

Consider: What is truth? Rene Descartes, the great mathematician and father of modern philosophy; Saint Augustine of Hippo, the great thinker of Christian antiquity; Saint Thomas Aquinas, the great medieval theologian; and Benedict de Spinoza, the foremost rationalist philosopher; all understood *truth to be the agreement of mind with reality.*

Furthermore, to understand truth, we must be able to assimilate, *validate,* and corroborate reality as it is, not as it might appear through speculation, a filter, or some optical illusion.

7

The simple fact of knowing it is painful to place a bare hand on a red-hot stove means more freedom from suffering.

Whether we comprehend the truth, or are subject to error, is determined by the fruits we produce. If we decide to place our hands on a hot stove, then our knowledge of hot stoves is obviously incomplete.

In addition, like balancing your checkbook, truth must be grasped not as a succession of simple facts, but in its *totality*—all at the same time.

Rene Descartes writes:

If, after we have recognized intuitively a number of simple truths, we wish to draw any inference from them, it is useful to run them over in a continuous and uninterrupted act of thought, to reflect upon their relations to one another, and to grasp *together* distinctly a number of these propositions so far as possible at the same time. For this is the way of making our knowledge much more certain, and of greatly increasing the power of the mind.[5]

YOU
ARE GREATER
THAN YOU KNOW

Consider the meaning of the second part of Jesus' words: Once you understand and know the truth, once you are able to make judgments that are in agreement with reality, you shall be free.

What does freedom in the cosmic sense mean? According to our present understanding, only the Creator is free—free from hunger, free from crisis, fear, worry, anger, and other human challenges. Is it possible that the Galilean is implying that we, too, are the Creator? That when we understand truth, we shall then be free?

History makes many subtle references to the divinity of man. Staggering insights into the godlike nature of man appear not only in the Gospels, but also in the writings of both modern and ancient sages, including Meister Eckhart, Aldous Huxley, Robert Muller, Walter Russell, William James, Shankara, Basil the Great, Pythagoras, and many others. However, because these advanced thinkers did not have the proper tools (not to speak of modern scientific research, investigation, and testing) for rapid, easy verification of their beliefs, many of their conclusions are still regarded as mere speculation.

We read in *The Encyclopedia Britannica:*

9

There are moments in the history of all sciences when remarkable progress is made in a relatively short period of time. Such leaps in knowledge result in great part from two factors: one is the presence of a creative mind—a mind sufficiently perceptive and original to discard hitherto accepted ideas and formulate new hypotheses; the second is the technological ability to test the hypotheses by appropriate experiments. The most original and inquiring mind is severely limited without the proper tools to conduct an investigation; conversely, the most sophisticated technological equipment cannot of itself yield insights into any scientific process. An example of the relationship between these two factors was the discovery of the cell. For hundreds of years there had been speculation concerning the basic structure of both plants and animals. Not until optical instruments were sufficiently developed to reveal cells, however, was it possible to formulate a general hypothesis, the cell theory, that satisfactorily explained how plants and animals are organized.[6]

Experiences of insight are not uncommon in our world. It is just that they are little spoken of. They encompass a variety of forms; some common, some extraordinary. One such experience clarifies what we are searching to share here:

I was sitting in the living room. It was an unusually quiet and peaceful Sunday evening. As daylight became twilight and finally turned into darkness, I continued to sit in my chair. As I sat, the street lamp in front of the house suddenly lit up. Its light broke the darkness of the room. I sat there transfixed by the glow of the light. Suddenly everything around me began to shimmer and glow with a pulsating light. It radiated a luminous whiteness from within the objects that surrounded me. The inner light *connected* everything that was in the room and outside with each other. I sat there for hours, feeling connected with all of nature to my soul, to every other person, to the cosmos. At some moment I found myself asking the question: "Why am I seeing this?" I heard from within me a gentle voice, "Because you are a part of it all, for all is light and thus love. And you are light and thus love too. We are One." Later that night I found myself searching endlessly through the Bible. I sought to find each and every passage that spoke of this light and love.

Our predecessors believed that a poorly understood relationship between God and man could be extremely dangerous and harmful in the wrong hands.[7] Therefore, they often concealed the deep significance of our position in nature in the symbolic language of delicately textured tales and parables, and in luxurious metaphors understandable only to one who truly knows all the ins and outs of the situation. This literature was, in a sense, *underground.* "In our literature," states *The New American Bible,* "we possess this literary form in the Negro spirituals; for example, 'Let My People Go.' The slaves sang it in their wooden, plantation churches: 'Tell de Pharaoh [the 'boss man' of the plantation] to let my people go.'"

Listen to the Galilean: "I assure you, there is something greater than the temple here" (Matt. 12:6). And again: "Do not give what is holy to dogs or toss your pearls before swine. They will trample them underfoot, at best, and perhaps even tear you to shreds" (Matt. 7:6). Furthermore, "To you the mystery of the reign of God has been confided. To the others outside it is all presented in parables, so that they will look intently and not see, listen carefully and not understand" (Mark 4:11).

We find a similar underground thought in the Hebrew *Sefer ha-zohar, The Book of Splendor,* a classic work of Jewish mysticism and one of the greatest expressions of the Kabbala:

> Woe to the man who sees in Torah [i.e., Law] only simple recitals and ordinary words! Because, if in truth it contains only these, we would even today be able to compose a Torah much more worthy of admiration. But it is not so. Each word of the Torah contains an *elevated meaning* and sublime mystery ... The recitals of the Torah are the vestments of the Torah. Woe to him who takes this vestment for the Torah itself! ... The simple take notice of the garments or recitals of the Torah alone. They know no other thing. They see not that which is concealed under the vestment. The more instructed men do not pay attention to the vestment but to the body which it envelops.[8]

The Jewish philosopher, jurist, physician, and foremost intellectual figure of medieval Judaism, Moses Maimonides, corroborates the Galilean and the Hebrew *Book of Splendor:*

> Every time that you find in our books a tale, the reality of which seems impossible, a story which is repugnant to both reason and common sense, then be sure that the tale contains a profound allegory veiling a deeply mysterious truth; and the greater the absurdity of the letter, the deeper the wisdom of the spirit.[9]

Saint Jerome, one of the most learned of the Latin Fathers and a biblical translator, reports: "The most difficult and most obscure of the holy books, Genesis, contains as *many secrets* as words, concealing many things even under each word."[10]

Saint Jerome's and Maimonides' beliefs are widely echoed in the writings of Papias, Justin Martyr, Irenaeus, Clement of Alexandria, Gregory of Nanzienzus, Gregory of Nyssa, and Ambrose. The most influential theologian and biblical scholar of the early Greek church, Origen, declares:

> What man of sense will agree with the statement that the first, second, and third days in which the evening is named and the morning, were without sun, moon, and stars, and the first day without heaven? What man is found such an idiot as to suppose that God planted trees in Paradise, in Eden, like a husbandman, and planted therein the tree of life, perceptible to the eyes and senses, which gave life to the eater thereof; and another tree which gave to the eater thereof knowledge of good and evil? I believe that every man must hold these things for images, under which the *hidden sense lies concealed.*[11]

And in *Selecta in Psalmos, Patrologia Graeca XII,* Origen explains:

> The Holy Scriptures are like houses with many, many rooms, and outside each door lies a key; but it is not the right one. To find the right keys that will open the doors, that is the great and arduous task.[12]

A scientist friend told me of his discovery of the right key for a particular door. He shared the following narrative:

> I was trying to understand how the universe is connected. When I started on the task many years ago it was as if I was traveling through a fog-filled swamp at night. As I traveled hip-deep in the weed-infested waters, it seemed at any moment that the bottom might drop away. Then would I be faced with struggling to stay afloat? But then again, what began to grow stronger was a hope, a conviction, that soon my feet *would* be on dry land.
>
> Suddenly I was no longer in a swamp but was seated at a desk surrounded by mounds of books. I was pulling equations from each of the different books. Each equation had different meanings. Each was a piece of the whole, of the One. Each was a *segment* of completeness.
>
> Then I saw the task. It was to first return to commonality and second to return to connectedness—to the relationship of the all in the all. And then, for the first time, I saw that it was not necessary to drop Einstein or Newton or any of the others. No, rather, they were now acceptable in the One. Days turned into months and the walls, ceiling, and floor became filled with equations ancient, medieval, and modern. I sat there with a great ball of string making connections from one equation to another. The room began to be transformed into a great inner web, a genetic code of stringed reality. The connections seemed limitless. It took seven years to make the connections and it took another ten to begin to understand them and their hierarchical structure—their bigness, their smallness, their sequence of more and more refined laws that describe the universe more and more accurately.

A CHILD'S STORY DECODED

Once, the greater danger was the harm done by a poorly understood truth in the wrong hands; today, the greater danger is in the harm done by a truth that is not recognized at all.

Science has bestowed a power on humankind which it has not yet learned to handle. Dealing with the risks has become the task of the century.

We see around us the stockpiling of conventional and nuclear weapons and the many crises in our system of values. Today we are witnessing an escalation of virtually thousands of national and international challenges. It has become increasingly important that the shining truth which all the myths and parables strove to hide and conceal from those not ready to receive them must now be communicated. And it must be verified by *You:* The truth is that *all is of the same essence, but in different states and forms — in different-sized containers.*

The Adam and Eve parable is one of many powerful passages in the Bible. It contains thoughts about the nature of man. Let us examine the Adam and Eve story in Genesis, before we proceed further:

1. Out of the ground the Lord God made various trees grow . . . with the *tree of life* in the *middle* of the garden and the tree of the knowledge of good and bad (Gen. 2:9).

2. The Lord God gave man this order: "You are free to eat from any of the trees of the garden, except the *tree of the knowledge* of good and bad. From that tree you shall not eat; the moment you eat from it you are surely doomed to die" (Gen. 2:16).

3. But the serpent said to the woman: "You certainly will not die! No, God knows well that the moment you eat of it *you will be like gods* who know what is good and what is bad." The woman saw that the tree was good for food, pleasing to the eyes, and *desirable for gaining wisdom.* So she took some of its fruit and ate it; and she gave some to her husband, who was with her, and he ate it. Then the eyes of both of them were opened, and they realized that they were naked (Gen. 3:4–7).

4. The Lord God said: "See! *The man has become like one of us,* knowing what is good and what is bad! Therefore, he must not be allowed to put out his hand to take fruit from the tree of life also, and thus *eat of it and live forever*" (Gen. 3:22).

5. He stationed the cherubim and the fiery revolving sword, to guard the way to the tree of life (Gen. 3:24).

Like a pot of gold, shining with a bright light over the centuries, this beautiful story from the Holy Bible is the Lord God's eloquent statement: "See! *The man has become like one of us,* knowing what is good and what is bad." Note this critical insight into our nature; we are freed through our capacity to know the truth, by our ability to make judgments that agree with reality. We become conscious by knowing good and bad; we create; we become Creators; we become God.

Both the Old and the New Testaments are rich mines of many similar stories. They reveal how we, like the Prodigal Son, may return home, a-chieve our potential, and partake in divine existence. The cryptic cipher of Israel's flight out of Egypt (the symbolic land of the fleshpots of sense enjoyment) is a priceless epic of the soul rather than mere historic record-ings. The Exodus story has its equivalent in the Mahabharata and the Ramayana of India. In the Book of Wisdom the ascension of Enoch and Elijah draws us into a life as sons and daughters of God, and, of course, the classic statement of our being sons of the Creator is brilliantly written in the Psalms: "*You are gods;* all of you are *sons* of the Most High" (Ps. 82:6).

Thales of Miletus, statesman, cosmologist, and discoverer of five geometric theorems in the sixth century B.C., gave us a pre-scientific Grand Unification Cosmology when he indicated: "All things are full of gods."

Our link with the Creator is confirmed by Christ: "Whoever has seen me has seen the Father" (John 14:9). Note the connection: anyone who has seen the Galilean has seen God. Jesus also said, "I am in the Father and the Father is in me" (John 14:11).

Just as the wave is a part of the ocean, so the ocean is a part of the wave, and so the Son of Man links himself to the same divine essence— the Father—the *Invariance,* that which doesn't change. Through physics and mathematics, we will see (refer to Appendix B, Table 2) that time is connected to space, space is connected to gravity, and *we are linked to them too.* We are a part of that Invariance—we are a part of God. We see this in the following: "I am in my Father, and you in me, AND I IN YOU" (John 14:20).

Ponder Christ's words. Reflect on their ramifications. They can change your life and the world around you. Is the Galilean right? Are we part of the same thing but in different states and forms? If we are, then the Creator is in us—in you.

John 14:20 is a monumental insight into the deepest nature of our Being. The Father is in the Christ and the Christ is in the Father—*"I am in you and you in me."* You are in the Father, and the Father is in you. You are in Christ and Christ is in you. *We are part of each other. We are part of one life.*

As physicist, Jesus revealed the processes and methodologies for understanding and modifying reality (creating miracles) through willing, visualizing end results, and knowing (feeling) in your heart that it is so (faith); dealing with the law of equilibrium through love, and so forth. Yet one of his greatest contributions is highlighted in John 14:9, 14:11, and 14:20. All of a sudden serving your neighbor, doing good, loving, and so on become *self-evident.* In particular, if you are aware (like placing your hands on a hot stove) that the neighbor you are giving the helping hand to is God—if he is You. Yes! You.

Erwin Schroedinger received the 1933 Nobel Prize in Physics for his wave equation that became the heart of modern quantum mechanics. Today, it is a widely used mathematical tool. He boldly remarks:

In Christian terminology to say, "Hence I am God Almighty" sounds both blasphemous and lunatic. But please disregard these connotations for the moment and consider whether the above inference is not the closest a biologist can get to proving God and immortality at one stroke.

In itself, the insight is not new. The earliest records, to my knowledge, date back some 2500 years or more. From the early great Upanishads the recognition ATMAN = BRAHMAN [the personal self equals the omnipresent, all-comprehending eternal self] was in Indian thought considered, far from being blasphemous, to represent the quintessence of *deepest insight* into the happenings of the world. The striving of all the scholars of Vedanta was, after having learnt to pronounce with their lips, really to *assimilate* in their minds this grandest of all thoughts. . . .

To Western ideology, the thought has remained a *stranger,* in spite of Schopenhauer and others who stood for it and in spite of those true lovers who, as they look into each other's eyes, become aware that their thought and their joy are numerical *one,* not merely similar or identical—but they, as a rule, are emotionally too busy to indulge in clear thinking, in which respect they very much resemble the mystic.[13]

Saint Paul makes a parallel link between the Creator and us: "In Him [in the Creator we are in Invariance or that which does not change] we live and move [we experience spacetime and relativity] and have our being [visible existence and matter]" (Acts 17:28).

Our world view has changed more rapidly in the last few decades than in any previous era in human history. The self-organizing "matter" has finally reached, through billions of years of evolution, a point of awareness where it is *beginning to know itself.* "A human being is a part of the whole," said Albert Einstein:

Called by us the "Universe," a part limited in time and space. He experiences himself, his thoughts and feelings as something separated from the rest—a kind of optical delusion of his consciousness. This delusion is a kind of prison for us, restricting us to our personal desires and to affection for a few persons nearest to us. Our task must be to free ourselves from this prison by widening our circle of compassion to embrace all living creatures and the whole of nature in its beauty. Nobody is able to achieve this completely, but the striving for such achievement is in itself a part of the liberation and a foundation for inner security.[14]

More recently, John Archibald Wheeler, the University of Texas astrophysicist, "packager" of the Black Hole concept, and a member of the American and National Academies of Sciences, stated: "The universe does not exist 'out there' independent of us. *We are inescapably involved in bringing about that which appears to be happening.* We are not only observers. We are participators."[15]

This statement is confirmed by another of the new physicists, D'Espagnot of France: "The notion of reality existing independently of man has no meaning whatsoever."[16]

Max Planck, who was awarded the Nobel Prize in Physics in 1918 for illuminating the path to modern quantum theory, predated both D'Espagnot and Wheeler when he said: "In the last analysis, *we ourselves are part of nature,* and, therefore, *part of the mystery that we are trying to solve.*"[17]

Abraham Isaac Kook, who was one of the most remarkable figures in the spiritual history of mankind, was Chief Rabbi of Palestine Jewry until his death just prior to the Second World War. Considered to be the foremost Jewish spiritual father of the twentieth century, he was also a prolific and eloquent author. He wrote:

> Special individuals, the sages of great understanding, always knew the secret of spiritual unity. They knew that the human spirit is a universal spirit, that although many divergences, spiritual and material, tend to separate person from person and society from society, greater than all the differences is the essential unity among them; that the processes of thought are constantly interacting, and ways of life tend to be harmonized. The objective of harmonization is surely to embrace the best, the healthiest and most sensitive in every society and to plant it on the soil of the larger human family.[18]

"I often feel as if my life were a lamp," shares former Assistant Secretary General of the United Nations, Robert Muller:

A temporary container filled with light, a flow of energy, condensed and held together for a little while in a mysterious, marvelous, living cosmos linked with the rest of the Earth and the heavens through material, touchable elements and immaterial, invisible elements. Some day the lamp will extinguish. The material elements will be reabsorbed by the Earth in its chains of life and energy. The immaterial elements will return to a universal *soul to be reborn in other forms on this planet or elsewhere in the universe. We are cosmic matter come alive, partaking of the divine character of our Creator.*[19]

Beauty wears more than one face. Time and again, the same enumeration appears. Time and again, the same fundamental truth is shown. Not only is the truth of who *You* are elucidated in one area, it is refracted, colored, and repeated according to the genius of the presenter throughout history and within the many processes of scientific inquiry.

MAN/WOMAN
BECOME
GOD

Note another deep truth from the Adam and Eve parable: "The man has *become* like one of us, *knowing* what is good and what is bad!" This disclosure presents a situation that existed prior to *becoming,* and prior to *knowing.* It concludes that before man really could understand the truth, he was not aware—he did not know—what was "good" and what was "bad."

He lived in fear—he fought *his* own being, like the left hand beating up the right hand. He was where we are today. But once he did—once man was able to make judgments that were in agreement with reality, he was free—he did not have to burn his own hand.

Do you hear the same insight from Christ and in Genesis? Do you see the same beautiful truth, lighted by a different lamp?

Furthermore, a statement of *becoming* also acknowledges a *colossal potential* in us. A tomato seed cannot grow into an oak tree, but an acorn can become an oak.

Similarly, "the man has become like one of us" shows man as the acorn, with the potential to transform—to make a *quantum* jump in awareness—to where he/she can know himself/herself as divine—*as one essence, but in different states and forms.*

In his Epistle to the Ephesians, Paul relates: "There was a time when you were darkness, but now *you are light* in the Lord. Well, then, live as *children of light.* Light produces every kind of goodness and justice and truth" (Eph. 5:8–9).

It's time to wake up now — to re-create the creation, amid the vastness of space and its billion trillion suns: "Awake, O sleeper, arise from the dead, and Christ will give you light" (Eph. 5:14).

Eighteen hundred years later, William Blake painted and wrote of life in its totality. He saw anew this unified image of the human being and its interconnectedness with the whole:

> *Awake! Awake O sleeper of the land of shadows,*
> *Wake! Expand!*
> *I am in you and you in me,*
> *Mutual in love . . .*
> *Lo! We are one.*[20]

Here is one more diamond in this cosmological treasure taken from the Psalms:

> *Rise, O God! judge the earth,*
> *for yours are all the nations (Ps. 82:8).*

The Galilean himself encouraged us to realize our "quantum" leap possibilities: "I solemnly assure you, the man who has faith in me will do the works I do, and greater far than these" (John 14:12).

Interestingly enough, even the serpent weaves this powerful message: "The moment you eat of it *you will be like gods* who know what is good and what is bad" (Gen. 3:4).

GOD
BECAME
WHAT WE ARE

The great contemplative and a leading Christian theologian of the second century, Saint Irenaeus, in his classic work *Adversus Haereses* boldly confirms our stunning ancestry and our cosmic road from Godhead to Godhead. His vision prefigures this path of leaving the *Invariance Plenum* by means of entering physical existence (including that of space and time) and finally our return again to the *Invariance Plenum*:

> God the Logos became what we are, in order that we may become what He himself is.[21]

In the fourth century Saint Athanasius, the chief defender of Christian orthodoxy, succinctly restated our great adventure and the transformation of "the self-creating universe" that lies ahead of us:

> *The Divine Word became man that we might become gods.*[22]

The rigorously analytical German quantum physicist Werner Heisenberg, who was awarded the Nobel Prize in Physics in 1932 for his brilliant Uncertainty Principle, states in *The Physicist's Conception of Nature:*

22

Here already we get a foretaste of the essential insight of modern physics stated with such impressive brevity by Eddington: "We have found that where science has progressed the farthest, *the mind has but regained from nature that which the mind has put into nature.* We have found a strange footprint on the shores of the unknown. We have devised profound theories, one after another, to account for its origin. At last, we have succeeded in reconstructing the creature that made the footprint. And *Lo! it is our own.*"[23]

Truly "the footprint on the shores of the unknown is our own." To those who have perceived their own nature—truly "We are a part of the mystery that we are trying to solve," as Max Planck said; and truly "I am in my Father, and you are in me, and I am in you," as Jesus said. Those who have not yet perceived their own nature must be given proper tools to enable them to conduct their investigation, testing, and verification.

Swami Rama in *The Book of Wisdom,* that is, *Kathopanishada,* writes:

The Vedic scriptures declare that the Brahman [Creator] became "Many" to realize its own glory and greatness. This manyness or plurality is but a transformation assumed by the Absolute which in its totality remains the One without a second. Parochial men make themselves mere toys in the hands of diversity. They go through this world of contingencies and delusions without gaining anything worth having. They create for themselves an eternal cycle of births and deaths from which they are unable to escape.[24]

The Upanishads portray a cosmic-egg cosmology before the "creation" of our universe and the Big Bang. They describe life before its excursion out of *non-being* (the Invariance Plenum) into the wild frontiers of physical existence (relativity plenum) filled with the *counting* and measurement of physical quantities. "In the beginning this world was merely non-being."[25] It was not the nothing from our familiar world of experience where an object suddenly appears out of nowhere; nor was it a Genesis paradox where the world started out in an emptiness, devoid of matter, of everything we see and experience.

Imagine leaving your living room for a second, going to the kitchen, and then, upon returning to the living room, finding it filled to the ceiling with gold, stock certificates, diamonds, and money! In daily life we expect everything to come from *something* or from *somewhere*. And so it does!

It is just the same with your home electronic calculator. It has the ability to count and to manifest the numbers zero through nine. Likewise, Nature has the potential to count and to manifest all the "numbers" (physical quantities, elements, molecules, human life, galaxies, and historical events). Nature is a dimensional slide rule of the physical laws that account for the smallest as well as the largest of realities. (See Appendix B and Table 6.)

However, the actual process of manifestation does not become visible until we start counting. *We must begin projecting patterns of excitation.* The state of non-being is the invariance condition (a zero or nothingness state, i.e. Table 6) in your electronic calculator's window. Before we begin counting, every number (manifestations of time, space, and physical law) is invisible. It is a condition *prior* to relativity and to the Big Bang, where the calculator begins to count. It is here the unfolding universe becomes apparent:

It *was* existent. It developed. It turned into an egg. It lay for the period of a year. [Then the Big Bang—and the spacetime counting begins.] It was split asunder. One of the two egg-shell parts became silver, one gold. That which was silver is this earth. That which was gold is the sky. What was the outer membrane is the mountains. What was the inner membrane is the cloud and mist. Where the veins were are the rivers; what was the fluid within is the ocean.[26]

The *Invariance Plenum* pervades everything. It is the ground of existence, and thus of everything we see and experience. It is timeless and motionless. It is invisible, undetectable and appears as *stillness* or *nothingness.* This ocean of stillness or nothingness, like the electromagnetic spectrum, has unique properties. In the electromagnetic spectrum, which is a subrange of the Invariance Ladder (see Page 155, and Table 7, Page 175), various *frequency* ranges bear different disguises and robes. Some wavelengths or frequencies, like various lengths of jumping rope, appear to our senses as sound, others as visible light or color, still others as heat. Similarly, in the Invariance or God the Logos Plenum, different ranges or excitation lengths (amounts) of nothingness (bundles of Invariance but in different size containers—strings and superstrings) like various currency coins, also bear different faces and robes. Some bundles of Invariance appear to us as time, others as space or matter, still others as beautiful women or handsome men. In physics, time, space and matter are termed physical quantities and have often been referred to in the Scriptures as membranes and egg shells.

We can also equate the "membranes" and "shells" of the Invariance Plenum to an electronic hand calculator's display window. Each calculator window has glass membranes on which the numbers are etched. The numbers are arranged in a fixed sequence and can be energized according to a predetermined formula. Note, although at a given moment one can display a particular number, each calculator window has a capacity to display other numbers in the same space.

Furthermore, just as the egg has a predetermined number of layers of egg-shells and yokes, and the hand calculator has a fixed sequence on which numbers are etched, so the smallest part of the Invariance Plenum has a fixed hierarchical sequence of quantities (please see Table II), elements (periodic table of elements), DNA and so forth.

The theoretical physicist and 1933 Nobel Laureate Paul Dirac was the instrument of many major breakthroughs. He devised a new form of quantum mechanics and developed a theory that predicted electron spin and the existence of the fundamental particle, positron. He introduced a quantum theory of radiation and was co-inventor of the Fermi-Dirac statistics. His work underscores in the twentieth century the ancient vision of creation in the Upanishads that matter is created out of non-being (nothingness):

All matter is created out of some imperceptible substratum and . . . the creation of matter leaves behind it a "hole" in this substratum which appears as antimatter. Now, this substratum itself is not accurately described as material, since it *uniformly fills all space and is undetectable by any observation.* In a sense, *it appears as NOTHINGNESS—immaterial, undetectable, and omnipresent.* But it is a peculiarly material *form of nothingness, out of which all matter is created.*[27]

25

The Bhagavad-Gita (*The Lord's Song*), composed by the great sage Vyasa, is the essence of India's vedic wisdom and one of the greatest and most beautiful of the Hindu scriptures. Henry David Thoreau wrote that in relationship to the *Gita*, "our modern world and its literature seem puny and trivial." The "theoretical physicist" and Hindu sage Vyasa, some twenty-five hundred years ago, went far beyond religious thought and ethical questions. He considered broadly, like our twentieth-century physicists Albert Einstein, David Bohm, Werner Heisenberg, Max Planck, Paul Dirac, Erwin Schroedinger, and others, *the Nature of God*—the *Nature* of Invariance, and the means by which men and women can know themselves.

Vyasa said:

All created beings are unmanifest [invisible like a film before its projection] in their beginning, manifest in their interim state [projected on the movie screen], and unmanifest [back on the shelf] again when annihilated.[2.28] [Furthermore] never was there a time when I did not exist, nor you, nor all these kings; nor in the future shall any of us cease to be.[2.12]

An equally beautiful articulation of Paul Dirac's perception is given by Lao-tzu (sixth century B.C.), the first philosopher of Chinese Taoism, in the *Tao te Ching*:

There is a thing inherent and natural
which existed before heaven and earth.
Motionless and fathomless.
It stands alone and never changes [is invariable];
It pervades everywhere and never becomes exhausted.
It may be regarded as the Mother of the Universe.
I do not know its name;
If I am forced to give it a name,
I will call it Tao, and I name it as supreme.[28]

About the same time as Lao-tzu's philosophical school and the religious brotherhood was being founded in China, Pythagoras of Samos (580–500 B.C.) was founding a movement in southern Italy (Croton).

Pythagoreanism believed in the divine origin and nature of the soul, and in the possibility of its rising to union (nothingness plenum) with the divine. Like Paul Dirac, David Bohm, Professor of Theoretical Physics at the University of London, gives us additional insight: How "God the Logos becomes visible" out of the *nothingness* plenum. It is by small patterns of excitation, like throwing photographic images onto a movie screen. It is like making projections onto a three-dimensional screen of reality:

> It is being suggested here, then, that what we perceive through the senses as *empty space is actually the plenum, which is the ground for the existence of everything, including ourselves. The things that appear to our senses are derivative forms and their true meaning can be seen only when we consider the plenum, in which they are generated and sustained, and into which they must ultimately vanish.*
>
> This plenum is, however, no longer to be conceived through the idea of a simple material medium, such as ether, which would be regarded as existing and moving only in a three-dimensional space. Rather, one is to begin with the holomovement, in which there is the *immense "sea" of energy described earlier.* This sea is to be understood in terms of a *multidimensional implicate order [Invariance], while the entire universe of matter as we generally observe it is to be treated as a comparatively small pattern of excitation. This excitation pattern is relatively autonomous and gives rise to approximately recurrent stable and separable projections into a three-dimensional explicate order of manifestation,* which is more or less equivalent to that of space as we commonly experience it.[29]

Twenty years ago, the Indian master Muktananda, during one of his discourses in New York, said, "God Himself assumes human forms and lives in the world."[30]

THE
CREATOR PLAYS
HIDE AND
SEEK

If you could, would you like to change your form from a human being to that of an ant? How would you like to live with ants, eat with them, and teach them a higher form of existence? Would you do it if you knew it would enable them to grow and evolve from being ants into human beings like yourself?

How much love for ants would this demand in your heart? How much love would be required if you knew that you were going to think like a human being in an ant's world? And how much love would be needed if you knew the ants were going to liquidate you for motivating them to become human beings? The Son of Man showed this love by his life. He left the Godhead and entered into dimensional multiplicity, *becoming man that we might become God again.*[31]

Furthermore, Christ's bold, brilliant, daring leap of loving genius ushers us, with the speed of tachian (faster than light) into a new frontier beyond that of General Relativity and beyond what Heisenberg referred to as the Uncertainty Principle. His life calls out for us to wake up and come to our senses. His life shows us that we have been living in a finite relativity world. He invites us to enter into a world of connected life: "[You] are not of the world any more than I belong to the world" (John 17:16).

His life tells us that we come out of that "imperceptible [nothingness] substratum . . . out of which all matter is created" as Paul Dirac put it in our earlier reference. We are "the ground for the existence of everything, including ourselves. The things that appear to our senses are derivative forms, and their true meaning can only be seen when we consider the plenum into which they must ultimately vanish," as David Bohm elaborated in our past citation.

"YOU ARE GODS" (John 10:34).
"YOU ARE THE LIGHT OF THE WORLD" (Matt. 5:14).

This is the truth Jesus strove so hard to convey. It is the mystery of our nature. It is the truth that sets us free. It is the truth by which *we are One and the same Essence* (John 14:20). It is that by which we are the same thing, formed in different containers of consciousness.

For two thousand years we have discussed and admired Christ's endless miracles and heroics. In reality they were meant to be frames for this Great Master Painting, dishes for the Great Feast of Life itself. It is now time for the marital celebration to begin. It is time to realize the unbroken wholeness of life's totality: "I assure you, as often as you did [give a cup of cold water] for one of my least brothers, you did for me" (Matt. 25:40).

Robert Muller, a native of Alsace Lorraine, reminded the members of the United Nations of this truth. He said:

> The soul of the universe, incarnated in a human being, lost much of its qualities and became imperfect. The effort of human beings should be to strive back to the perfection of the soul and to feel part of the mysterious flow and throbbing life of the universe.[32]

The medieval mystic professor Meister Eckhart, of Cologne, gave joyful form to Muller's striving for "the perfection of the soul," David Bohm's "multidimensional implicate order," and Paul Dirac's "undetectable and omnipresent" *nothingness* substratum through dimensional multiplicity of time, space and matter. Eckhart lived in the world, and he thought, spoke, and acted with the aid of symbols in order to preserve the first forms of the Invariance Plenum of the Godhead. He said:

When I came out of the Godhead into multiplicity, then all things proclaimed, "There is a God." Now this cannot make me blessed, for hereby I realize myself as creature. But in the *breaking through* I am more than all creatures; I am neither God nor creature; *I am that which I was and shall remain, now and forevermore.* There I receive a thrust which carries me above all angels. By this thrust I become so rich that God is not sufficient for me, insofar as He is only God in his divine works. For in thus breaking through, I perceive what *God and I are in common.* There I am what I was. There I neither increase nor decrease. For there *I am the immovable which moves all things.* Here man has won again what he is eternally and ever shall be.[33]

Ninety years ago, the head of the Department of Philosophy at Columbia University, John Dewey, described this leap of intelligence into the movement of life:

Intelligence has descended from its lonely isolation at the remote edge of things, whence it operated as *Unmoved Mover,* and ultimate good, to take its seat in the moving affairs of men.[34]

Figure 1 presents the comparative nomenclature and the cycle of life, from God to Man and Man to God, as it has been described by the world's leading thinkers, scholars, and scientists. Also, in Appendix A you will find a Summary of Insights with references to the four states: I Invariance, II From God to Man, III Relativity, IV From Man to God.

The Summary of Insights can be a useful tool for anyone desiring to study each of the areas separately. After reading the main portion of this book, you might find it helpful to review them. They were designed to give you an integrating insight into my basic sense of who we are and where we are heading.

Why would one wish to forget the superlife of the Invariance, of the Ultimate Reality? Why would one sail forth on a mythic voyage to the dimensional multiplicity of legendary and enchanted places in our modern world? Why are we called to live in a world of fast-moving, atom-smashing particles, string theories, multinational banks, theater,

Comparative Nomenclature and the Cycle of Life

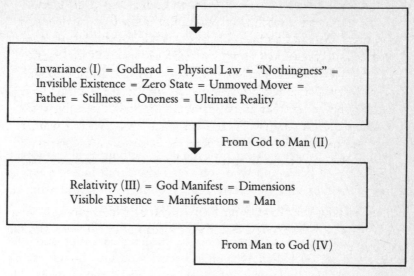

Figure 1

dance, political powwows, sushi-to-go shops, biotechnology, fascinating games of lawmaking, parliamentary management, astrophysics, and tiny space probes into the more than one billion galaxies of our observable universe? Why are we asked to depart from Paul Dirac's imperceptible "nothingness substratum" in order to live in the midst of the spectacular Big Bang fireworks, with large-scale, cosmological structure and planet-forming, multicellular organisms, the search for antigravity, interlocking shareholdings, and more? Why are we called out to stir the depths of our nature, to color our memories with love and desire? Why are we asked to place such a desperate wager on this limited, earthly life?

There you are, *alone* across the many dimensions and universes, for billions and billions of years. All alone in your ivory tower, withdrawn from sight, separated from seductions, strifes, and strains; divorced from the everyday tasks of cooking, cleaning, shopping, and supporting others emotionally. You live without mate or sweetheart, without someone to talk to . . . to share with . . . There is an absence of the challenges of personal finance, product management, sales goals. There is nothing to do.

You are an Unmoved Mover. You are in touch with everything in space and time. *You are aware of yourself.* You know all that was, is, or ever will be. You know all of history and *can* predict precisely both the location and the momentum of a particle at a given moment, like a prerecorded movie. You know it from beginning to end. There is nothing further to be discovered. There is nothing more to be revealed. You are speaking of yourself to yourself. Even constant bliss and mathematical virtuosity seem boring.

Wouldn't you make a change? Maybe do something as silly as forget everything you know and who you are? How about hiding yourself from yourself in some supernova, tall mountain, beautiful woman, handsome man, or dark bluebird with pretty red eyes?

Let's leave this view of the never-changing (invariable) Divinity. Let us contemplate our entrance into the created order and our appearance as 100 billion subatomic particles or suns in the earth's galaxy. Let's play hide and seek with ourselves through many un-related worlds, such as self-organizing forms of *the united states of nature,* colored quarks, curvature-tensors, AAAS's, AMA's, royal societies, churches, multinational corporations and governments, and galaxies of intelligent civilizations engaged in equally intelligent conversations.

Let's ponder such practical questions as: How do we prevent nuclear war? How do we discover corporate *excellence,* greater productivity? How do we cut medical costs, attain peak experience and fulfillment? Once immersed back in this world, how long will it take us in our temporary spacetime Disneyland pajamas, to discover our roots, who we truly are once again?

It takes us quite a while to "regain from nature that which the mind has put into nature," according to the Nobel Laureate Eddington. Following are some of the steps that return us to undivided totality:

When I was a galactic cluster,
I did not know;
When I was a neutron star,
I did not know;

When I was a salty ocean,
I did not know;
When I was a mighty sequoia,
I did not know;
And when on my way I became a beautiful woman,
I still did not know;
But, when I let Christ's teachings (purity of heart, love, and peace)
Be my life,
I realized that I am, was,
And shall always be the Absolute Reality.

Yes, we can rediscover this first consciousness and learn with Meister Eckhart that "I am that which I was and shall remain, now and forever more."

"Oh human blindness!" laments the remarkable woman Saint Teresa of Avila, whose wisdom came without formal schooling and whose acclaim came to her in spite of never aspiring to public fame, "How long, how long shall it be before the dust is removed from our eyes?"[35] How can our minds assimilate this grandest of all thoughts—"You [are] in me and I am in you" (John 14:20)—that all of us are *the same One Essence?* How are we to experience the feelings and understandings that come to us from being at one with our Creator, from being with, in, and through our Creator, from being Co-Creators, from being Creators?

TO FIND
THE CREATOR,
OUR MINDS MUST
BE STILL

According to people who find their way homeward to the Oneness Plenum—to grasp truth, as Rene Descartes recommended, "together"—as one—all "at the same time," it is crucial that *the mind be still* and that *the heart be loving and pure.*

Note that a mere knowledge of food does not help a hungry person. Similarly, it is not enough to know intellectually the principles of purity of heart or stillness of mind. They must be experienced directly if we are to perceive who we are. Without this, David Bohm's unbroken wholeness will be unattainable.

We must remember that what we want to *experience* or *empirically verify* is *invariable.* It is unchangeable, immovable. It is Paul Dirac's "nothingness." It is complete stillness. It is the plenum out of which all matter is created. "It is through resting one's mind at ease that Buddhahood is realized," sings Jetsun in his *One Hundred Thousand Songs of Milarepa.*[36]

Through radio or television reception, we tune in to the desired frequency of the program we wish to receive. (Please refer to Figure 2.) But when tuning into the Invariance Plenum, to Bohm's multidimensional implicate order of the physical law, which is unchanging, immovable, and invisible, and which supports all frequencies in the

34

changing, moving, and visible world, we must *tune* our intellect to *stillness.* We must inhibit thought.

The mind must be completely still. Our brain neurons must tune in to the self if we are to achieve *self-realization.* We must tune into the uncreated order if we are to realize the created one. We must experience a peace and quiet within ourselves that is the only verification of that naked truth that grasps the totality of things, of the unity of all in all.

Chuang Tzu, the fourth-century B.C. Chinese sage, said, "A man does not see himself in running water but in still water."[37]

Radio, TV, or Relativity Tuning

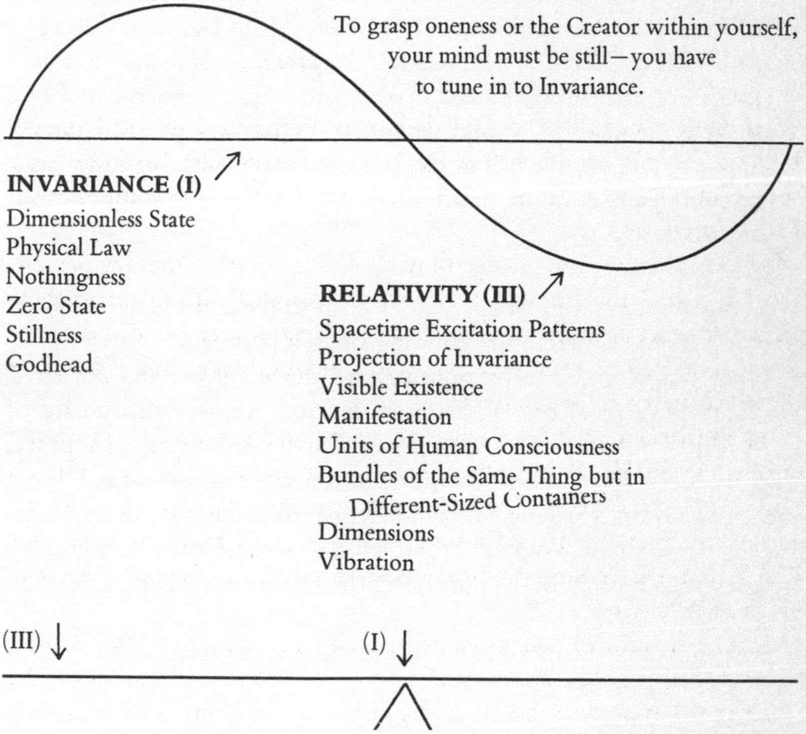

To grasp oneness or the Creator within yourself, your mind must be still—you have to tune in to Invariance.

INVARIANCE (I)
Dimensionless State
Physical Law
Nothingness
Zero State
Stillness
Godhead

RELATIVITY (III)
Spacetime Excitation Patterns
Projection of Invariance
Visible Existence
Manifestation
Units of Human Consciousness
Bundles of the Same Thing but in
     Different-Sized Containers
Dimensions
Vibration

(III) ↓   (I) ↓

Figure 2

35

In the nineteenth century the social reformer Edward Carpenter presented methods and processes whereby the inhibition of thought tunes us in to the Invariance Plenum (please refer to Figure 2) and verifies the central truth of who we are:

> Of all the hard facts of science, I know of none more solid and fundamental than the fact that if you *inhibit thought* [and persevere], you come at a region of consciousness below or behind thought . . . and a realization of an altogether vaster self than that to which we are accustomed. And . . . the ordinary consciousness with which we are concerned in ordinary life is before all things founded on the little local self, and is in fact self-consciousness in the ordinary self and the ordinary world. It is to die in the ordinary sense, but in another sense, it is to wake up and find the "I," one's real, most intimate self, PERVADES THE UNIVERSE AND ALL OTHER BEINGS . . . So great, so splendid is this experience, that it may be said that all minor questions and doubts fall away in face of it; and certain it is that in thousands and thousands of cases the fact of this having come even once to a man has completely revolutionized his subsequent life and outlook on the world.[38]

What does purity of heart have to do with stillness of the mind? What does it have to do with understanding oneself better?

When our attitudes and actions toward our neighbor and our environment are carried out with unselfish love, we act with purity of heart. When our conscience—our friend down inside of us—is at peace, then we are at peace. Our perception and awareness increases. Loving unselfishly is like cleaning the windows of our house; it allows us, by passing through the windows of our soul, to see and understand reality by being one with it. In the pure heart the subject and object are one in love.

We can reduce purity of heart to a mathematical relationship:

$$
\begin{aligned}
\text{purity of heart} &= \text{clear thinking (wisdom, intelligence)} \\
&= \text{ability to make better decisions (reason, judge)} \\
&= \text{perception of truth (understanding)}
\end{aligned}
$$

36

Hence, just as energy is directly related to mass, so purity of heart is directly related to clear thinking and better decision making. *The greater the purity of heart, the better the judgment,* and conversely, the less the purity of heart, the poorer the reasoning.

Recall Christ's statement in his Sermon on the Mount: "Happy are the pure in heart; they will *see* God!" (Matt. 5:8 GN), and "Know the truth, and the truth will set you free" (John 8:32). But God is truth and truth is God. Therefore, *happy are the pure in heart for they will SEE the truth, and the truth will set them free* is not only true, but it is also a breakthrough formula to a higher level of freedom and understanding of who we are and how we relate to everyone else.

Every great teacher worth his or her salt always started with love and ended with love. For love not only allows for a more orderly functioning of society; it is also the gateway to your own and other people's hearts and minds.

WHEN HEART
SPEAKS TO HEART,
WHAT MORE
IS THERE TO SAY?

Although most of us instinctively know what love is, Og Mandino shares with us in one of his beautiful scrolls, from *The Greatest Salesman in the World:*

I will greet this day with love in my heart.

For this is the greatest secret of success in all ventures. Muscle can split a shield and even destroy life, but only the unseen power of love can open the hearts of men, and until I master this art, I will remain no more than peddler in the market place . . .

And how will I do this? Henceforth will I look on all things with love and I will be born again. I will love the sun for it warms my bones; yet I will love the rain for it cleanses my spirit. I will love the light for it shows me the way; yet I will love the darkness for it shows me the stars. I will welcome happiness for it enlarges my heart; yet I will endure sadness for it opens my soul. I will welcome obstacles for they are my challenge.

I will greet this day with love in my heart.

And how will I speak? I will applaud mine enemies and they will become friends; I will encourage my friends and they will become brothers. Always will I dig for reasons to applaud; never will I scratch for excuses to gossip. When I am tempted to criticize, I will bite my tongue; when I am moved to praise, I will shout from the roofs . . .

I will greet this day with love in my heart.

And how will I confront each whom I meet? In only one way. In silence and to myself I will address him and say, "I love you." Though spoken in silence, these words will shine in my eyes, unwrinkle my brow, bring a smile to my lips, and echo in my voice; and his heart will be opened. And who is there who will say nay to my goods when his heart feels my love?

I will greet this day with love in my heart.

And most of all I will love myself. For when I do I will zealously inspect all things which enter my body, my mind, my soul, and my heart. Never will I overindulge the requests of my flesh, rather I will cherish my body with cleanliness and moderation. Never will I allow my mind to be attracted to evil and despair, rather I will lift it with the knowledge and wisdom of the ages. Never will I allow my soul to become complacent and satisfied, rather I will feed it with meditation and prayer. Never will I allow my heart to become small and bitter, rather I will share it and it will grow and warm the earth.

I will greet this day with love in my heart.

Henceforth will I love all mankind. From this moment all hate is let from my veins, for I have not time to hate, only time to love. From this moment I take the first step required to become a man among men. With love I will increase my sales a hundredfold and become a great salesman. If I have no other qualities, I can succeed with love alone. Without it I will fail though I possess all the knowledge and skills of the world.

I will greet this day with love, and I will succeed.[39]

Saint Paul, in his first letter to the Corinthians, nineteen hundred years ago, put the excellence of the gift of love thusly:

Now I will show you the way which surpasses all the others. If I speak with human tongues and angelic as well, but do not have love, I am a noisy gong, a clanging cymbal. If I have the gift of prophecy and, with full knowledge, comprehend all mysteries, if I have faith great enough to move mountains, but have not love, I am nothing. If I give everything I have to feed the poor and hand over my body to be burned, but have not love, I gain nothing. Love is patient; love is kind. Love is not jealous, it does not put on airs, it is not snobbish. Love is never rude, it is not self-seeking, it is not prone to anger; neither does it brood over injuries. Love does not rejoice in what is wrong but rejoices with the truth. There is no limit to love's forbearance, to its trust, its hope, its power to endure (1 Cor. 13:1–7).

EXPERIENCE
IT!

Make purity of heart, love, and peace your own. Quiet your mind. Quiet your soul. Be STILL with your whole being. *Concentrate on inner peace* and nothing else. Just as in the *center of an electromagnetic wave* (Figure 2), peace in our mind creates a *zero state.* Energies in our body, like electrical power or water falling from the top of a mountain, start rushing towards the *lowest* energy level (the electrical zero ground potential), thus producing a regenerative and uplifting effect.

In this loving embrace and timeless bliss of stillness, *you will be slowly filling up your mind and body with bioplasma energy.* (More on this later.) Your awareness will quicken and will begin to break out of the chains of your present consciousness. This is how the distinction between you and your surroundings will slowly disappear.

You will perceive, like Albert Einstein, David Bohm, Erwin Schroedinger, John Archibald Wheeler, Werner Heisenberg, Paul Dirac, Max Planck, Robert Muller, and many others, the unity of the universe. Time, space, from here to there, and everywhere in between will become One, like one light merged in the ocean of light.

You will then see that you and the rest of reality, large and small, are part of one and the same splendor and stillness, one and the same joy of conscious glory and light. You will transcend bliss, anticipation, and desire. You will, as

Rene Descartes recommended, "grasp together distinctly a number of these propositions so far as possible at the same time." You will be in nirvana. (Note: *ni* in old Buddhist scriptures means "no" and *rvana* means "broken.") The state of nirvana is David Bohm's multidimensional implicate order of unbroken wholeness—oneness. In this state, says Chuang Tzu quite simply, "I and all things in the Universe are one."

Why should it not be so, questions the German Dominican Henry Suso: "All creatures . . . are the same life, *the same essence,* the same power, the same one and nothing less."

It was not so long ago that a friend of mine was faced with a challenge. He was trying to build a computer that would simulate the effects of atomic explosions. How could he compute a large series of numbers, not in a linear way, one after another, but in their totality— through *parallel* addition? He narrates the incident:

> Unexpectedly 100 computer processors appeared in front of me. I saw in the vision the internal makeup of a parallel electronic machine designed to add a new 100 problems to the old 100 problems. I picked up my pen and began to transcribe the *mathematical equations* that I *saw* in front of my eyes. Upon completion, I turned over the plans for the machine to be built and patented. It was built, patented, and it worked. Today every high-speed computer uses this parallel carry look-ahead principle in its computation.

In his masterpiece of psychological interpretation, *The Varieties of Religious Experience,* William James, Harvard professor of anatomy, physiology, psychology and philosophy, who was a practical, cash-value, result-and-profit-oriented pragmatist, writes about overcoming the illusionary barriers:

> This overcoming of all the usual barriers between the individual and the Absolute is the great mystic achievement. In mystic states we become one with the Absolute and we become aware of our oneness. This is the everlasting and triumphant mystical tradition, hardly altered by differences of clime or creed. In Hinduism, in Neoplatonism, in Sufism, in Christian mysticism, in Whitmanism, we find the same recurring note, so that there is about mystical

utterances an eternal unanimity which ought to make a critic stop and think, and which brings about what the mystical classics have, as has been said, neither birthday nor native land, perpetually telling of the unity of man with God, their speech antedates language, and they do not grow old.[40]

In William Blake's grand superglimpse, "If the doors of perception were cleansed, everything would be seen as it is, infinite."[41]

George Santayana, who did his research under William James at Harvard College, and in 1889 joined the faculty of philosophy, sounds the calling truth: "I do not ask anyone to think in my terms if he prefers others. Let him *clean* better, if he can, the windows of his soul, that the variety and beauty of the prospect may spread more *brightly* before him."

Father, let them find the road to the unity of the universe, prayed the Nazarene. Let them find out that "I am in you, Father, and you are in me, Father, and that we are in them, Father." Let them move closer toward the cosmic Invariance Plenum and happiness:

> *That they may be one, as we are one—*
> *I living in them, you living in me—*
> *that their unity may be complete* (John 17:22).

And Saint Paul, in his second epistle to the Corinthians, explains his new unified image of the human being: "All of us . . . are being transformed *from* glory *to* glory into his very image by the Lord who is the Spirit (2 Cor. 3:18).

"Actually," says the theoretical physicist Erwin Schroedinger,

> One can say in a few words why our perceiving self is nowhere to be found *within* the world-picture: because it itself is the world-picture. It is identical with the whole, and, therefore, cannot be contained in it as a part.[42]

He is absolutely right! Just as we cannot have a reflection in a mirror without an image, so we also cannot have relativity (manifestation, reflection, projection) without the Invariance (image).

43

That is, the *reflection* "is identical with the whole," as Schroedinger said, for "it itself is the projection of the world-picture," i.e., projection of Invariance.

"Reality is only one and that is the Self," confirms Ramana Maharshi:

All the rest are mere phenomena in it, of it and by it. The seer, the objects and the sight, all are the Self only. Can anyone see or hear, leaving the self aside? . . . If you surrender yourself . . . all is well . . . Only so long as you think that you are the worker, are you obliged to reap the fruits of your actions. If, on the other hand, you surrender yourself and recognize your individual self as only a tool of the Higher Power, *that Power will take over your affairs along with the fruits of actions.*

You are no longer affected by them and the work goes on unhampered. Whether you recognize the power or not, the scheme of things does not alter. Only there is a change of outlook. Why should you bear your load on the head when you are travelling in a train? It carries you and your load whether the load is on your head or on the floor of the train. You are not lessening the burden of the train by keeping it on your head but only straining yourself unnecessarily. Similar is the sense of doership in the world by individuals.[43]

On another occasion Maharshi expounded on the difference between the kingdom of heaven and our body—between what is within us and what is outside us:

The sense of "I" pertains to the person, the body and brain. When a man knows his true Self for the first time, something else arises from the depths of his being and takes possession of him. That something is behind the mind; it is infinite, divine, eternal. Some people call it the kingdom of Heaven, others call it the soul, and others again Nirvana, and Hindus call it Liberation; you may give it what name you wish. When this happens, a man has not really lost himself; rather he has found himself. Unless and until a man embarks on this quest of the true Self, doubt and uncertainty will follow his footsteps through life. The greatest kings and statesmen try to rule others when in their heart of hearts they know that they cannot rule themselves. *Yet the greatest power is at the command of the man who has penetrated to his Inmost depth,* ... What is the use of knowing about everything else when you do not know yet who you are? Men avoid this inquiry into the true Self, but what else is there so worthy to be undertaken?[44]

"To live with the true consciousness of life centered in another is to lose one's self-important seriousness and thus to live life as 'play' in union with a Cosmic Player," repeats the monk Thomas Merton. He writes:

It is He alone that one takes seriously. But to take Him seriously is to find joy and *spontaneity* in everything, for everything is gift and grace. In other words, to live selfishly is to bear life as an intolerable burden. To live life *selflessly* is to live in joy, realizing by experience that life itself *is love* and a gift. To be a lover and a giver is to be a channel through which the Supreme Giver manifests His love in the world.[45]

LET THE
GALACTIC FIRE
BURN

The *garden,* vineyard, or field, in the symbolic language of the parables, represents our *body,* our physical vehicle, while the man or gardener stands for the Deeper Self, the driver of the vehicle.

In Genesis we find, "God then took the man and settled him in the Garden of Eden [placed the Deeper Self within the body of Eden, that is, paradise, delight, pleasure] to cultivate and care for it" (Gen. 2:15).

The *fruit* symbolizes our actions and their actual reward, product, or fruit. Jesus states, "By your fruits you shall be known"—by the achievement of your work you shall be recognized. *Eating* fruit from the tree of life and knowledge signifies our *internal* consumption of the fruit. How can we internally consume something (the tree of life) that imparts life, wisdom, and knowledge?

We know from literature that the seed of life, (the "heavenly fruit" of pure pleasure, the lifeforce, the nirvana fruit, the bioplasmic biological high energy) is life-giving and is involved in the process of life propagation. We also know that in organic evolution there is a process of natural selection and procreation through sexual energies. Thus it appears from Genesis that there is something to look forward to . . . There is a bonus. Based on our performance and accomplishments, somehow we can

46

consume this heavenly fruit and thus our knowledge, wisdom, and understanding will improve.

On the surface this idea sounds strange. Yet upon further deliberation it is clear that there is an internal capacity within each species that helps it grow and transmits its genetic life-code to future generations. Scores of rich and diverse books have been written on this subject. You may want to explore these particular biological bases for improving consciousness, vitality, health, and inner peace. I strongly recommend that the bioplasma (kundalini) areas be investigated.

I have verified the existence of these internal biological systems. They ensure our advancement to the new cosmic frontiers of development. They are within us for us to realize our exceptional abilities, greater happiness, and to achieve reunion with the Godhead. Through proper development, one can experience the *redirection* of the subtle essence of bioplasma energy (the procreative energy of the genital center) from what Lady Yeshe Tsogyel, a remarkable eighth-century Tibetan called "the secret center, where bliss is preserved," to the crown of the head to enable one to perceive who one really is.

When we experience momentary sexual climax or orgasm, *very minute* amounts of our procreative and creative energy reach, through a small electrification conductor in our back, to the top of our head. The majority of the cosmic seed essence, however, using our current *stone age knowledge* about sex, is diverted and discharged to the exterior.

In more advanced *union* or *creative synthesis* with sustained rapture, ALL of the life-force of love can be kept and utilized *internally* (to elevate oneself to a higher plateau of existence; to *propel* oneself faster through reality; to quickly manifest what one desires) by circulating it inside our body; that is, from the reproductive area up through a very large electrification conductor (the central channel) in our body, to our head (for creation of powerful thought forms), then down through the heart to the base of the spine, and up to the top of the head again.

Thus, during the more evolved embrace and bliss of nirvana, where sexual joy is not cut short by lack of self-control and higher purpose, literally thousands of thermonuclear orgasms and climaxes can last, *without interruption,* for many hours. *None* of the seed essence is discharged to the outside ("guard the very essence of pleasure," advise teachers of tantra). But conversely, as both of you are consciously *circulating* the

47

life-force in resonance in your bodies, the bioplasma energy starts filling up your billions of cells with the subtle essence of the generative force, producing one giant Big Bang rapture after another, with tremendous intensity and duration.

Here, in this divine creative synthesis of celestial ecstasy, where we can make the sacrament of sexual union literally produce miracles (create new realities) for us, all melts into One. Like one light merged in the ocean of light, you transcend the outermost bounds of anticipation and desire. You reach a fountain of delight and peace so overpowering that it exceeds all other joys that we might have experienced to this point, and surpasses all understanding.

What is more, the new *intensified* and *elevated* bliss of creative splendor, instead of depleting the husband and wife physically, mentally or emotionally, electromagnetically connects the male and the female into a *single* married being. It actually becomes a stunning *LIFE CHARGER* and energy booster. Furthermore, one experiences an ultimate *high of much greater magnitude and duration than normal sexual experience.* Here the old stone age climax becomes almost repulsive—a pale shadow in the face of thousands of blazing suns.

Moreover, the transmuted bioplasma energy serves as a Rosetta stone and *amplifier* of our awareness, vitality, creativity, and thought processes. It illumines this reality's shrouded darkness, literally providing a miracle wand to *sharpen the mind,* practical insight, health, happiness, and prosperity.

Here finally, in the creative synthesis of *luminous* electromagnetic fields, the sexual union allows one to come out of the dark caves of need, fear, crime, sickness, hunger, and war. We soar very rapidly in peak performance, wisdom, mental and paranormal capacities, cosmic consciousness, exceptional altruism, and an armada of other capabilities, enabling us to create whole new realities and ways of more abundant living.

Parts of a very advanced science and technology aimed at *elevating* oneself on the ladder of reality to the defying heights of a Sky Dancer (a mystical term for a female Buddha, God) are disclosed by Tsogyel:

Unite male and female energies,
Developing the method of MIXING higher and lower energies,

Female assisting male and male assisting female,
The principle of each being separately practiced.
Intensify and *elevate* your practice,
Broadening the horizons of your pleasure;
But if pleasure and emptiness (peace and stillness of the mind)
Are not experienced,
Profitlessly you stray from the path of *unfoldment:*
Apprehend the intrinsic unity of pleasure and emptiness . . .
PRACTICE TO PERFECTION THE SKILL OF
RETAINING YOUR SEED–ESSENCE;
Or you will become like ordinary men and women;
Without energy control your sexual activity is fornication;
If seed-essence is *lost* in actuality
The karma of *slaying* a Buddha is incurred;
At all costs gain self-control.[48]

At all costs do not abuse the core of your being, or drain your energies of Light and Life. At all costs practice to perfection the retention of your seed essence. At all costs help to develop the God within you.
 Another deep truth from this female Bodhisattva:

United at your consort's blissful nerve,
Our two nectars fused into one elixir.
The phenomena of self and the others extinguished,
Awareness won you the Initiation of Creative
Expression.[49]

Then she weaves into the creative tapestry the common sense fire:

Through an effortless method of pure pleasure . . .
The bond is formed.
You are the bond!
The bond is all!
The bond is strong.
Let the fire burn!
We are burning together!
Thus . . . [we] were joined, and we entered a trance of *union*.[50]

49

The Gospel of Thomas is an anthology of 114 sayings of Jesus. Comparable in importance to the Dead Sea Scrolls, it was one of the most remarkable and inspiring archaeological finds of our time. In it, the Galilean brings to light how the union of male and female creates a stunning new *awareness* and quality of being (becoming a single one). These teachings provide a quantum advancement for our understanding of the kingdom within:

> When you make the male and the female *into a single one,* so that the male will not be male and the female not be female . . . then shall you enter the Kingdom.[51]

In the *Zohar* we find more corroboration on the spiritual fusion:

> Every soul and every spirit coming into this world is composed of a male and female *united in one being.* Descending to earth, these two halves separate and go off to animate different bodies. At the time of marriage, the Holy One, blessed be He, Who knows all souls and spirits, unites them as before, and *they become again a single body and a single soul.* . . . But this union is consistent with the actions of man and the way he has traveled. If he is pure and behaves piously, he will enjoy a union exactly like the one that preceded his birth.[52]

The Gospels of Matthew (19:1) and Mark (10:6), as well as *The Gospel According to Thomas,* quote Jesus presenting a story similar to that of the *Zohar:*

> At the beginning of creation God made them male and female. For this reason a man will leave his father and mother and be united to his wife, and *the two shall become as one.* They are no longer two but one flesh (Mark 10:6–8).

In Revelation, Saint John assures us that the person victorious in Christ-like selfmanagement skills also consumes the fruit that flourishes in the garden of God:

I will see to it that the victor [the one who transmutes vices into virtues] *eats* from the *tree of life* which grows in the garden of God (Rev. 2:7).

And in chapter twenty-two of the Book of Revelation we read: "Happy are they who wash their robes . . . to have free access to the tree of life and enter the city through its gates!" (Rev. 22:14)

YOUR
SEED OF
PURE PLEASURE

How do we liberate these powerful living energies of love, creativity, happiness, and success? How do we *purify* our bioplasma seed essence? How can larger quantities (twenty to fifty times the normal production) of the enchanting seed essence be more effectively channeled *upward* in our body?

The Adam and Eve story doesn't elaborate on the actions that precipitate this "nectar fruit" being liberated, purified (separating the poisonous seed essence from the pure seed essence) and consumed in larger quantities. But many great thinkers and physicians of the human soul the world over, including Buddhists, Christians, Hindus, and Taoists, suggest that this is accomplished through a transfiguration of the interior universe. They each speak of this transformation being accomplished through a life of love, purity of motive, *doing your best each day,* detachment from results, stillness of the mind, fasting, and service.

Dr. Robert Muller of the United Nations presents a simple plan for us:

Decide to live joyfully,
exultantly, gratefully, openly,
and then miracles will begin to happen.[53]

Alexander Kelly McClure, an intimate friend of Abraham Lincoln, who during the Civil War saw the President almost daily and was at once his confidant and advisor, writes:

> Of all the Presidents of the United States, and indeed of all the great statesmen who have made their indelible impression upon the policy of the Republic, Abraham Lincoln stands out single and alone in his individual qualities. . . . He was patient, tireless, and usually silent. . . . When he reached his conclusion, he was inexorable. . . . His judgment of men was next to unerring, and when results were to be attained, he knew the men who should be assigned to the task, and he rarely made a mistake.[54]

When asked, Abraham Lincoln attributed his success to the following:

> I have never had a policy. I have simply tried to *do what seemed best each day,* as each day came . . . I desire so to conduct the affairs of this administration that if at the end, when I come to lay down the reins of power, I have lost every other friend on earth, I shall at last have one friend left, and *that friend shall be down inside of me.*[55]

"Live as much as may be in the eternal,"[56] said Harvard's George Santayana. "Your inability to drink the nectar [seed of pure pleasure]," suggests the Tibetan Prince of Light, Milarepa, "was because your Central Channel was not yet opened. You should practice certain vigorous bodily exercises."[57]

The great sage Ashtavakra, who, like Albert Einstein, saw the path as being "in the service of mankind,"[58] in his famous book, *Ashtavakra Samhita* (which is not recommended for beginners) warns his royal disciple (King Janaka):

> . . . not to rest content with mysticism, ordinary yoga, or religion alone, but to take the further step necessary to acquire a know-ledge of the philosophy of truth — not to flee to caves or sit idly in ashrams but be constantly engaged in work for the welfare of others.[59]

Yes, nothing happens until someone makes it happen. We are asked to see, judge, and act. In our minds and hearts, we have the power to choose the best. In our hands, we have the power to do the best. We are called to see clearly and to choose the good that we see.

Shankara, who in the ninth century systematized the philosophy of the Upanishads and *The Bhagavad-Gita,* summarizes in his *Viveka-Chudamani,* that is, *The Crest-Jewel of Wisdom:*

> Disease is not cured by pronouncing the name of medicine, but by taking medicine. Deliverance is not achieved by repeating the word *Brahman,* but by directly *experiencing* Brahman. . . . The nature of the one Reality must be known by one's own clear spiritual perception; it cannot be known through a pandit [learned man]. Similarly, the form of the moon can be known only through one's own eyes. How can it be known through others?[60]

The Gospel of Saint John says: "If you live according to *my* teaching, you are truly my disciples; then you will *know* the truth, and the truth will set you free" (John 8:31–32).

The Gospel of Saint Thomas declares: "Love your brother as your own soul, guard him as the pupil of your eye."[61]

Why such a strict requirement? Why must our actions be in tune with inner peace, with common sense, with Christ's way of seeing before we can experience the profound change of perspective and realize the unbroken wholeness of totality? Why must we appreciate that *sexual intercourse creates a permanent spiritual bond of marriage* (having nothing to do with legal marriage)? For like hydrogen and oxygen (that *electromagnetically* unite to become water), the two people become *one* through the sacrament of sexual love. The Christian gospels, the Jewish *Zohar,* the *Koran,* and the sacred books of the East underscore this. Furthermore, each time a *new* marriage is established, we not only connect ourselves to that person's electromagnetic network, but, like mixing many paints, acquire from that network the idiosyncrasies of the other's personality and the people they are connected to.

Why do we have to honor the ways of love and *purity of ONE marriage?* Why do we have to *purify* our bioplasma seed essence before we can tap the thermonuclear orgasm of the tree of life and knowledge?

First, to raise ourselves, so to speak, to a higher energy level, we must *invest* in happiness—in life. We cannot increase the quantity and quality of tomatoes until we prepare the soil, eliminate weeds, and take care of the plant. We cannot increase the *quantity* and *quality* of our precious life energy supply to the high levels of spiritual service if we decide to live wastefully and thoughtlessly. Furthermore, if, during the course of our sex act, this energy is discharged because of premature lust, we are slaying the Buddha (God) as Tsogyel discloses. We diminish our *brain, heart,* and *will power.*

In addition, each time we "connect" ourselves with someone new in a sexual relationship, we put another *energy drain* on our souls. Having many different sexual relationships is like having an oil pipeline with many people siphoning off the flow along its length. By an internal consumption, in large quantities, of our "seed of pure pleasure," we are *unlocking* the centuries-old secrets of the power, happiness, creativity, and wisdom of our greatest human achievers.

Moreover, this tremendously powerful cosmic energy must be used constructively, for *productive* endeavors, for the advancement of our consciousness, wisdom, health, joy, and prosperity. In anger, fear, tension, worry, or misdirection of our life-force, the negative energy is very *stressful* on our mind and our body. This can even lead to many stress-related illnesses, including ulcers, heart attacks, and insanity.

Remember when the Galilean, in anger, projected negative energy on the fig tree? It died the next day. Imagine the same force projected inward. World literature has many similar examples.

Luckily, when we get angry, fearful, or upset, in most cases, in our present stage of development, we do not channel much life-force to our mind (our "Central Channel has not opened yet," as Milarepa says), therefore, we do not do much damage to our surroundings or ourselves, except for such minor maladies as headache, upset stomachs, lower back pain, or nervous tension.

Life must protect itself. There is a margin of safety. Through pain, hunger, and suffering, You the Creator are "gently" guided, like the Prodigal Son, *homeward* to happiness and inner peace again. For this reason, as in an atom bomb, there are various safety measures and locks in our body ("He stationed the cherubim and the fiery revolving sword, to *guard* the way to the tree of life"—see chakras below) which will not open the central channel (the large electrical conductor for our nirvana fruit) of the tree of knowledge until we have achieved a high degree of goodness and purity of heart.

The *serpent*[62] represents existence, wisdom, and life—the power that puts physical, mental, and emotional life in motion. The bioplasma energy is coiled like a serpent at the base of the spine. Since the sperm (whose head, like a serpent's, is pushed forward by a highly efficient system of propulsion—the undulating movement by a long, slender tailpiece) looks like a serpent, those who saw it in stillness gave it a very good name.

A similar symbol was used by the early people of Meso-America (Coatl, the serpent) in association with life and the transformation of man into light; by the Chinese; by the Egyptians (the serpent on Pharaoh's head); by the wise Nagas of Hindu literature; by Moses; and by the Nazarene. In the East the serpent represents the awesome power of kundalini, the seed of pure pleasure, or "the serpent power," and it is referred to in the Bible as the bread from heaven, or the seed.

"A character which plays a great role in the story of Adam and Eve is the Serpent," writes Edouard Schure in his study of the secret history of religious symbols:

> Genesis calls it *Nahash*. Now what did the serpent mean in the ancient temples? The mysteries of India, Egypt, and Greece reply with a single voice: the serpent arranged in a circle means universal *life,* whose magical agent is starlight. In a still deeper sense, *Nahash* means *the power which puts life in motion,* the attraction of the self for self. In the latter meaning Geoffrey Saint-Hilaire saw the basis for universal gravity. The Greeks called it Eros, Love, or Desire. Now apply these two meanings to the story of Adam and Eve and the Serpent, and you will see that the Fall of the first couple ... suddenly becomes the vast revealing of divine and universal nature with its kingdoms, its classes and its species, in the tremendous, ineluctable *cycle of life.*[63]

MANY THOUGH
WE ARE, WE
ARE ONE
BODY

As the transfiguration of our interior universe—through a life of excellence, purity of heart, purity of marriage, detachment, and stillness of mind—towards the Godhead begins to take place, minute amounts (without the sexual act) of bioplasma are released. They ascend (like the sap in a tree) through a large electrification conductor in our body to the top of our head, *electrifying* and *amplifying* (illuminating) the consciousness circuitry to the brain to such a degree that one begins to *realize* that he or she is part of the one indivisible reality, that all are one living interconnection.

Initially, the state of this rapturous experience is momentary, with exhilarating joy and exaltation. Later on, as we grow, as we become more Christ-like (Buddha-like, Krishna-like) in our behavior, attitude and sensitivity towards our family, co-workers, and environment, *the Central Channel* (the Hindus call it *shushumna*) *begins to widen, allowing greater amounts of our life-force energy to pass through it.* The exhilarating joys become more frequent and of longer duration (lasting for hours), extending even into sleep. And eventually, as the interior development, under the Spirit's direction, progresses over the years, we achieve a very powerful connection with our Deeper Self—we realize that we are the Creator itself. "We begin to realize," writes Wingate in his *Tilling the Soul:*

That we are joined in the most deeply intimate communion with every other Soul in the Cosmos. That we are joined with the One Soul. That It is in us. That we and the One Soul are One. And we begin to realize who and what the One Soul really is: No longer are we bogged down by the teachings and dogmas of an age when it was believed that the Universe was only 3,000 years old and 3,000 miles in diameter. Now we are free to experience the One Soul in whatever way It needs to manifest Itself to us, in whatever way It needs to reveal Itself to us, for us to be able to understand It and accept It.[64]

Nineteen centuries earlier, Saint Paul presented our multinational connection thusly:

We, many though we are, are *one* body (1 Cor. 10:17)

and,

We are members of one another (Eph. 4:25).

Yes, corroborates Carey in *Vision:*

The Creator and Creation are joined in physical flesh; for it is One Life that pulses within every body. We have now only to be joined in consciousness, in awareness, and all will be fulfilled according to the prophecy.[65]

Circulating internally, through meditation or in love par excellence, large amounts of bioplasma can produce an electrifying experience and bliss thousands of times greater than a normal sexual climax or orgasm. The Bible tells us that Moses at first "flees the serpent" (Exod. 4:3). But once the bioplasma is under control—"Put out your hand and take hold of its tail," (Exod. 4:4)—the bioplasma becomes a source of common sense, joy, innovation, and staying power. It helps you knock down barriers and remove blinders to what is possible. You electromagnetically connect your brain's neural antenna, your will, and your feeling (heart) power to *internal* guidance from your Deeper Self.

As Saint Paul testifies in the First Epistle to the Corinthians, "The kingdom of God does not consist in talk but in power" (1 Cor. 4:20). Likewise, the kingdom does not exist in living in pain, hunger, or self-destruction, but in the power to heal, to create, to produce new wonders, and to be the light to each other. As Jesus reminds us: "All that the Father has is yours."

"How true," strikingly illuminates Wingate:

Call Me Omega
Or God, or Jehovah, or Brahma, or Allah,
Or anything else you would like to call Me.
I AM all of these. Yet I AM also none of them.
I AM the Cosmos, the Universe. Everything That Is . . .
I AM the First Cause.
I AM the Last Effect.
I AM Every Cause and Every Effect.
I AM Spirit.
I AM Soul.
I AM Matter.
As Spirit, I AM the inexpressible, indefinable Source of All Being,
    infinite and eternal.
As Soul, as Spirit manifest for an Evolution,
I AM Mind. I Am Consciousness. I AM Beingness. And as
Matter, as Soul manifest for a lifetime,
I AM Everyone and Everything.
I AM Perfect, and Every Cause and Every Effect and
Everyone and Everything are Part of My Perfection.
I AM THE ONE.
I AM ALSO THE MANY.
AND WHATEVER IT IS THAT SAYS I AM,
I AM THAT I AM.[66]

Gopi Krishna, who studied the impact of bioplasma on people in India, Tibet, China, Japan, and the Middle East, and who himself experienced kundalini, attests:

Probably no other spectacle, not even the most incredible super-normal performance of mystics and mediums, so clearly demonstrates the existence of an All-Pervading, Omniscient intelligence behind the infinitely varied phenomena of life as the operations of a freshly awakened kundalini. It is here that man for the first time becomes acutely aware of the staggering fact that this unimaginable Cosmic Intelligence is present at every spot in the Universe, and our whole personality, ego, mind, intellect, and all—is but an infinitely small bubble blown on this boundless ocean.[67]

THE
AWAKENING
OF THE
SELF

The Christian mystics, without perhaps being aware, experienced the effects of kundalini through meditation. They use phrases similar to those used by kundalini practitioners, such as "the wine of pure pleasure."

For example, Saint Teresa of Avila stated, "the raptures . . . carry the soul out of its senses."[68] It "penetrates the very marrow of your bones."[69] Your senses can be fused into one ineffable act of perception. Differences between time, space, and motion will cease to exist.

Each one of us can find ourselves in the center of a stillness and immersed in a living glow so pronounced that the distinction between ourselves and our surroundings disappears. We discover we are ONE with the rest of our surroundings in the same light and stillness, in shimmering, conscious joy, happiness, and love. It can happen when we are quiet or active.

It is an experience of life in its most fantastic, indescribable, and delightful splendor. It is authentic peace, beyond thought and emotion, where we cease to exist as separate entities and become a part of one infinite and loving Reality.

For there we can dive into the ocean of knowledge, where the basic concepts of science, technological inventions, and works of art are removed from obscurity and instantaneously become clear to us. This is a method par excellence by which problems can be solved quickly and hidden truth can be known with the speed of light. This shining knowledge of existing things above and beyond all empirical reason, beyond all discursive thought, is nearer to us than we are to ourselves, when our neural antennae and innermost circuitry are tuned into our Deeper Selves.

"This is the way," Saint Catherine of Siena's inner voice said to her while she was in this elevated state:

> If you will arrive at a perfect knowledge and enjoyment of Me, the Eternal Truth, you should never go outside the knowledge of yourself; and by humbling yourself in the valley of humility you will know Me and yourself, from which knowledge you will draw all that is necessary.[70]

Saint Teresa of Avila, who drank "the wine of pure pleasure," similarly relates in her meditations:

> There will suddenly come to it [the soul] a suspension in which the Lord communicates most secret things, which it *seems to see within God himself.* . . . The brilliance of this vision is like that of infused light or of a sun covered with some material of the transparency of a diamond . . . For as long as such a soul is in this state, it can neither see nor hear nor understand; the period is always short and seems to the soul even shorter than it really is. God implants Himself in the interior of that soul in such a way that, when it returns to itself, it cannot possibly doubt that *God has been in it and it has been in God.*[71]

Saint Catherine of Genoa, whose discourses parallel those of Basil the Great, was one of the most penetrating gazers into the secrets of Eternal Light. She wrote:

> When the loving kindness of God calls a soul from the world, He finds it full of vices and sins; and first He gives it an instinct for virtue, and then urges it to perfection, and then by infused grace

leads it to true self-naughting, and at last to true transformation. And this noteworthy order serves God to lead the soul along the Way; but when the soul is naughted and transformed, then of herself she neither works nor speaks nor wills, nor feels nor hears nor understands, neither has she of herself the feeling of outward or inward, where she may move. And in all things it is God Who rules and guides her, without the mediation of any creature. And the state of this soul is then a feeling of such utter peace and tranquility that it seems to her that her heart, and her bodily being, and all both within and without is immersed in an ocean of utmost peace; from whence she shall never come forth for anything that can befall her in this life. And she stays immovable, imperturbable, impassible. So much so, that it seems to her in her human and spiritual nature, both within and without, she can feel no other thing than sweetest peace. And she is so full of peace that though she press her flesh, her nerves, her bones, no other thing comes from them than peace.[72]

Recall the Adam and Eve narrative: "The moment you eat from it you are surely doomed to die." But why have they not died? The answer is that they have, but only figuratively. They died as natural people, and were reborn in awareness as Sons of the Creator.

The eyes of both of them were opened and in cosmic consciousness they saw the naked truth: that we are God! ("The Lord God said, *'See! The man has become like one of us...!'*") When the planted seed dies, something much more grand, a new beautiful plant, is born.

GLORIFY
THE CREATOR
IN YOUR
BODY

Paul, from Tarsus in Cilicia, a staunch defender of the old traditional God, who arrested, imprisoned, and persecuted men and women to the point of death (Acts 22) also had his eyes opened to the light of this very penetrating insight:

> Are you not aware that you are the temple of God and that the Spirit of God lives in you? . . . For the temple of God is holy, and *you* are that temple (1 Cor. 3:16–17).

He is right! The Creator is not limited to any particular place, church, ashram, or temple, but is present EVERYWHERE—throughout nature and within us! Yes, says the Bible, "*Your* body is a temple of the Holy Spirit, who is within" (1 Cor. 6:19).

Saint John wrote, "God is love and he who abides in love abides in God, and God in him" (1 John 4:16). Thus to experience the abundance of life for ourselves and to truly serve others with excellence, we need to live the words of Saint Paul, "Glorify God in *your* body" (1 Cor. 6:20).

Yes! Strangely, we are called to become that which *we already are*: "The kingdom of God is within you." In the created order we have assumed *many forms of physical reality*—forms of time, space, gravity, matter, atoms, and elements. We have clothed ourselves in stars, galaxies, and history. We are walking the streets of New York, London, Tokyo, and Moscow. We don't recognize ourselves in the other beings. And within them we are called to return home to one Glory—to the Godhead, to our Greater Self.

A friend of mine shared this experience with me:

> I was waiting for my wife and children on a bench in Disneyland, Florida. People were rushing from one fantasy ride to another. A man sat next to me and we exchanged a few words. He was also waiting for his family. He told me who he was—the Creator lost in the matter of our universe. He understood oneness. Then we just sat in silence. His family came. We got up, hugged, and parted. I saw an indescribable light on his face. There was great joy in my heart in the midst of Donald Ducks, Mickey Mice, and fantasy rides. I found a soul who knew his roots. At that moment I felt that I had found a "human being" after many wanderings through the woods of birds, fishes, and bears. And there was great joy.

Teilhard de Chardin challenged us to live this life when he announced:

> Someday after mastering the winds and the waves, the tides, and gravity, *we shall harness the energy of love*. And then, for the second time in the history of the world, man will have discovered fire.

This is the love of the flaming sword of Israel. This is the love of the fullness of knowledge given witness to by the Hebrew cherubim.

The fiery revolving sword, which looks like a compressor of a spinning jet engine, is a high energy transformer[73] or the "lotus guard" that protects our "fruit of pure pleasure" from prematurely being released into our body. But it is also the chakra of the Hindus', of the Buddhists', and of the Egyptians' "Gateway reserved for Gods." The fire is our heavenly fruit of pure pleasure. The fire is the authentic conductor of the dancing energies of creativity for those who have achieved a high degree of inner peace and stillness of the mind.

In the symbols of the story of Adam and Eve, we see an expression of these eternal truths related to the unlocking of the highest energies of self-illumination and spiritual evolution.

Certain Biblical passages point to this reality indirectly, in a cryptic code language:

> The reign of God is like a *buried* treasure [within you] which a man found in the field. He hid it again, and rejoicing at his find went and sold all he had and bought that field (Matt. 13:44).

In other places the Scriptures say it directly:

> Is it not written in your law, "I have said, 'YOU ARE GODS' "? If it calls those men gods to whom God's word was addressed—and Scripture cannot lose its force (John 10:34–35).

The Psalms convey the same prayerful direction:

> They know not, neither do they understand; they go about in darkness; all the foundations of the earth are shaken. I said: "You are gods, all of you, sons of the Most High" (Ps. 82:5).

In Galatians we find:

> You are my children, and you put me back in labor pains until Christ [God] is formed [realized-matured] in you" (Gal. 4:19).

This is your true destiny! This is our cosmic truth. The kingdom of God is within all of us. In *The Gospel of Thomas,* Jesus presents us with a statement of how complete this divine intimacy is:

> *The Kingdom is within you*
> *and it is without you.*
> When you know yourselves,
> then you will be known
> and you will be aware that you are
> the sons of the Living Father.
> But if you do not know yourselves,

then you are in poverty
and you are the poverty.[74]

Furthermore,

Let him who seeks not cease from seeking until he finds;
and when he finds,
he will be disturbed,
and when he is disturbed,
he will marvel,
and he shall reign over ALL.[75]

On the surface, *The Gospel of Thomas* appears a little cryptic. Together let us do some decoding in light of what we know:

1. Let one who seeks the truth—who seeks God—not stop searching until one finds what one is looking for; until one discovers God within oneself.

2. When one ascertains this truth, one will become distressed and question why it took one so long to find the precious truth of Who One Is. *For all this time you were me and I was you and we did not know it.*

3. One then begins to experience the awe and thanksgiving that life is wonderful and each of us is everywhere.

4. Finally, after all the marveling, each of us will, in the words of Einstein, "place [our] powers freely and gladly in the service of mankind"[76]—then we shall reign over all.

The great Hindu sage Vyasa spoke of this in the language of his time, as Albert Einstein and David Bohm speak to us today, in the language of our time. *The Bhagavad-Gita,* that is *The Lord's Song* states:

There is no other-thing-than I in truth . . .
Everything rests upon me,
As pearls are strung on a thread—
I am the taste of water,
The light of the sun and the moon,
The syllable OM in the Vedic mantras;

67

I am the sound in ether and the ability in man.
I am the original fragrance of the earth,
And I am the heat in fire.
I am the life of all that lives,
All states of being—
Be they of goodness, passion or ignorance—
Are manifested by My Energy,
I am, in one sense, Everything.[77]

Rejoice, my beloved! You are also looking at yourself through your brother's eyes!

The Hindu scripture Chandogya Upanishad, which aims to describe the origin, nature, and destiny of man and his universe, assures us that we don't have to go far to find our Creator: "This whole world is Brahma"[78] and "Atman alone is the whole world."[79]

Truly:

YOU ARE HE.[80]—I Myself am he![81]
The world is his; indeed, he is the world itself.[82]

And more corroboration:

Verily, this Soul is the overlord of all things, the king of all things. As all the spokes are held together in the hub and felly of a wheel, just so in this Soul all things, all gods, all worlds, all breathing things, all these selves are held together.[83]

And in his Epistle to the Galatians, Saint Paul communicates this fundamental concept:

Each one of you is a son of God . . . (Gal. 3:26).

Ken Wilber, in his book *Quantum Questions,* which deals with the writings of the world's greatest physicists, brings this two-thousand-year-old message of the Epistle to the Galatians into the present:

All things, including subatomic particles, are ultimately made of God.[84]

David Bohm spent forty years researching the physics and philosophy of this statement at the Lawrence Radiation Laboratory in Berkeley and during his appointments at Princeton, the University of Sao Paolo, and Haifa. He wrote:

> The entire universe [with all its "particles," including those constituting human beings, their laboratories, observing instruments, etc.] *has to be understood as a single undivided whole,* in which analysis into separately and independently existent parts has no fundamental status.[85]

The Svetasvatara Upanishad presents one more breath-taking insight:

> *Thou art woman. Thou art man.*
> *Thou art the youth and the maiden too.*
> *Thou as an old man totterest with a staff.*
> *Being born, thou becomest facing in every direction.*
> *Thou art the dark blue bird and the green parrot with red eyes.*
> *Thou hast the lightning as thy child.*
> *Thou art the seasons and the seas.*
> *Having no beginning.*
> *Thou dost abide with all-pervadingness.*
> *Wherefrom all beings are born.*[86]

Some twenty-five centuries later, Ken Carey offered this validation:

> *I beat with every throb of your heart,*
> *Feel with every touch of your hand,*
> *Cry your every tear,*
> *Breathe your every breath.*
> *I am never far away.*[87]

Saint Bernard shares with us a similar treasure:

Who is God? I can think of no better answer than *He who is.*
Nothing is more appropriate to the eternity which God is. If you
call God good, or great, or blessed, or wise, or anything else of
this sort, it is included in these words, namely He is.[88]

Mahatma Gandhi, who used the weapons of love, non-violence, and
morality against political, social, and military destructive forces, saw
the presence of God in all beings. For him the path of liberation was
that of the love of all creatures, the ethics of self-discipline, and the
work of *selfless service:*

> To me God is Truth and Love, God is Ethics and Morality. God is
> fearless. God is the source of light and life and yet He is above and
> beyond all these. God is conscience. He is even the atheism of the
> atheist. He transcends speech and reason. He is a personal God to
> those who need His touch. He is the purest essence. He simply *is*
> to those who have faith. He is long suffering. He is patient but He
> is also terrible. He is the greatest democrat the world knows, for he
> leaves us unfettered to make our own choice between evil and
> good. He is the greatest tyrant ever known for he often dashes the
> cup from our lips and under cover of free will leaves us a margin so
> wholly inadequate as to provide only mirth for himself at our
> expense. Therefore, it is what Hinduism calls all this sport—Lila,
> or calls it an illusion Maya.[89]

This is just as true for the Moslem Sufis:

> *The 'world' is but forgetfulness of God;*
> *It is not spouse and child, silver and gold.*
> *Who from this world did turn his face away,*
> *He was not lost; indeed, instead, he found*
> *His long-forgotten and lost Self again.*
> *No bar guards His palace-gateway,*
> *No veil screens His Face of Light—*
> *You are my heart! By your own self-ness,*
> *Are enwrapped in darkest night.*[90]

The Irani Avatar Merwan Sheriarji, known as Meher Baba, in his discourses explains:

> There is only one question. And once you know the answer to that question, there are no more to ask. . . . Out of the depths of unbroken Infinity arouse the Question, Who am I? And to that Question there is only one Answer—*I am God!* The problem is that people do not know who they really are: You are Infinite. You are really Everywhere; but you think you are the body, and therefore consider yourself limited. If you look within and experience your own soul in its true nature, you will realize that you are infinite and beyond all creation.[91]

For this is the joy of Christ consciousness:

> *I am in your own souls!*
> *Why see you not?*
> *In every breath of yours am I,*
> *But you are blind.*
> *Without true eye,*
> *And see Me not.*[92]

And still another insight.

> *He who is absent, far away from God—*
> *His heart can only say: "God is," somewhere;*
> *He who has found the Loved One in Him-Self—*
> *For him God is not he, nor You, but I.*
> *Whom may I take for guide upon the Way*
> *One who himself away from it does stray?*
> *He is content to say "God is," while I*
> *Am desolate till I "God am" can say!*[93]

These pearls of wisdom are endless. Eventually when all of us find God within ourselves, we will compose similar insights:

If you find God, then you have found all things!
Just think! If the Creator you do find.
Can His creation still remain behind?
Is the One ever separate from the Other?
"Indeed I am this All, All This is Mine"—
This word resoundeth ever from within!
You are Your-Self the Thinker, and this world
But Your own Thought, and God but
Your-Self.[94]

Our finest investment as businessmen will not be found in searching worldwide for management firepower, liquidity, restructurings, corporate profitability expectations, interest rates, integrity of the dollar, inflationary breakouts, and high technology investment selections. We do not first need high-speed computers, up-to-date information on monetary supply, global markets, including Eurobonds, mortgage-backed securities, in-bond indexing and interest-sensitive stocks.

The greatest and finest investment is in ourselves. The greatest return to be made is on that treasure that lies within each of us. The Hindu Vedanta states:

Why will you wander in the wilderness!
You who are seeking God!
Yourselves are He!
You need not search!
He is you, verily![95]

Tukaram Maharaj said, "I went to look for God, but didn't find God. *I myself became God.* In this very body, God revealed Himself to me."

The Old Testament Psalter states:

They know not; neither do they understand;
they go about in darkness;
all the foundations of the earth are shaken.
I said: "You are gods;"
all of you are sons of the Most High;
Yet like men you shall die,

and fall like any prince.
Rise, O God, judge the earth,
for yours are all the nations (Ps. 82:5–8).

And *Tasawwuf* reiterates:

The wise see in their heart the face of God,
And not in images of stone and clod!
Who in themselves, alas! can see Him not,
They seek to find Him in some other spot.[96]

Hui Neng says, "When non-enlightened Buddhas are no other than ordinary beings; when there is enlightenment, ordinary beings at once turn into Buddhas."[97] Erwin Schroedinger, who studied self-realization among the mystics, puts it this way:

Again, the mystics of many centuries, independently, yet in perfect harmony with each other [somewhat like the particles in an ideal gas] have described, each of them, the unique experience of his or her life in terms that can be condensed in the phrase: DEUS FACTUS SUM; that is, "I have become God."[98]

Their descriptions differ but they share in a *fundamental truth* that the Upanishads state simply:

Cows are of many different colors,
But the milk of all is one color, white;
So the proclaimers who proclaim the Truth
Use many varying forms to put it in,
But yet the Truth enclosed in all is One.[99]

Once a high degree of "purity of heart" is achieved, our limited thoughts about ourselves are removed. We begin to understand, at first hazily, and later quite lucidly, that true joy is not to be found somewhere out there or somewhere deep under one's skin, but rather it is blazing forth from all of us. *"Truly, You are Godhead Yourself"*[100].... "He Is You," as Vedanta proclaims. And there is no one else!

73

It is most moving and chilling that this includes Stalins, Hitlers, and Mao Tse-Tungs, as well as the millions they destroyed. It includes all of history's Saviors, Machiavellies, evil comedies, high technologies, and banana republics; for we and our brothers and sisters are one and the same Being. *"We are members of one another."* (Eph. 4:25) "All are one in Christ Jesus," (Gal. 3:28) as the Bible proclaims. All share in the same celebration of joy, happiness, and ONEness.

Understanding this beautiful eternal ONEness is not so simple. Our mind's bio-electronic circuitry, similar to that of the universe, is subject to physical laws. It is very difficult to propel a fifty-ton truck through a two-inch hole. The same applies to our mind's neural-antenna. The truth is that the kingdom of God is within each and every one of us; we are all one; we are of the same essence—but in different-sized containers. This awareness is so immense and our mind's opening is so small that although this message has been clearly and splendidly presented century after century, even today most men and women cannot grasp it.

If we did penetrate into the mind of God, we would not be brooding in the darkness of some desperate isolation or alienation. We would not be holding onto the absolute boundaries between Jews, Hindus, Buddhists, Christians, and Moslems. There would be neither a *Mein Kampf* nor a *Book of Mao.* The Dachaus, Vietnams, and fifty thousand nuclear bombs would not exist. There would be no murders, rapes, robberies, or sicknesses.

James Jeans, who made fundamental contributions to the dynamic theory of gases, the mathematical theory of electromagnetism, the nature of nebulae, and the evolution of gaseous stars, states:

> Things are not what they seem; it is the general recognition that we are not yet in contact with ultimate reality. We are still imprisoned in our cave, with our backs to the light, and can only watch the shadows on the wall.[101]

ALL
IS YOU:
THE VERY
SAME ESSENCE

"Whatever came to be in him found life," states the Gospel according to John, "life for the light of men; THE LIGHT SHINES on in darkness, a darkness that did not overcome it" (John 1:4–5).

"It is because we don't know Who we are," reveals Huxley in *The Perennial Philosophy:*

> Because we are unaware that the Kingdom of Heaven is within us, . . . that we behave in the generally silly, the often insane, the sometimes criminal ways that are so characteristically human. We are saved, we are liberated and enlightened, by perceiving the hitherto unperceived *good* that is already within us, by returning to our eternal ground and remaining where, without knowing it, we have always been.[102]

"A man has many skins in himself, covering the depths of his heart," says Eckhart von Hochheim:

> *Man knows so many things;*
> *He does not know himself.*

Why, thirty or forty skins or hides,
Just like an ox's or bear's,
So thick and hard, cover the soul.
Go into your own ground
And learn to know yourself there.[103]

Yes, shares *Theologia Germanica*, "Goodness needeth not enter into the soul, for it is there already, only it is unperceived."[104] "The Beloved is all that lives."[105] [For] "all are one" (Gal. 3:28), "One body and one spirit" (Eph. 4:4)—*All is you, the very same essence* and Being, but only in different containers—different packages, states, and forms that must be directly experienced by you.

As the Bible relates:

> The body is one and has many members, but all the members, many though they are, are one body. . . . Now the body is not one member, it is many. If the foot should say, "Because I am not a hand I do not belong to the body," would it then no longer belong to the body? If the ear should say, "Because I am not an eye I do not belong to the body," would it then no longer belong to the body? If the body were all eye, what would happen to our hearing? If it were all ear, what would happen to our smelling? As it is, God has set each member of the body in the place he wanted it to be. *If all the members were alike, where would the body be?* There are, indeed, many different members, but one body. The eye cannot say to the hand, "I do not need you," any more than the head can say to the feet, "I do not need you" . . . If one member suffers, all the members suffer with it; if one member is honored, all the members share its joy. You, then, are the body of Christ. Every one of you is a member of it (1 Cor. 12:12–27).

The Vedas give us a similar perspective:

> The countless heads, eyes, ears, and hands and feet of living beings are all parts of One Man.[106]

Or another magnificent insight:

The progeny of Adam, all are parts
And limbs of one and the same organism,
Risen from the Same Essence, everyone;
And can it be, while one limb is in pain,
That other limbs should feel at restful ease?[107]

"This that I am now uttering unto you," reveals the founder of Islam, Muhammad:

The Holy Quran—it is to be found
Within the ancient Seers' writings too;
For Teachers have been sent to every race.
Of human beings no community
Is left without a warner and a guide.
And aught of difference we do not make—
For disagreement there is none.
Between these Prophets. All that have been sent,
Have been so sent but One Truth to proclaim—
"I, verily the I All-One, am God,
There is no other God than I (the Self,
The Universal all-pervading Self),
And I alone should be adored by all.[108]

No community is left without a wake-up bugler and a guide to proclaim the good news of our roots and heritage—to wake up all of us from our long sleep. But "Mind is patient," says Freeman Dyson, professor of physics at the Institute for Advanced Study in Princeton:

Mind has waited for three billion years on this planet before composing its first string quartet. It may have to wait for another three billion years before it spreads all over the galaxy. I do not expect that it will have to wait so long. But if necessary, it will wait. The universe is like a fertile soil spread out all around us, ready for the seeds of mind to sprout and grow. Ultimately, late or soon, mind will come into its heritage.

What will mind choose to do when it informs and controls the universe? That is a question which we cannot hope to answer. When mind has expanded its physical reach and its biological organization by many powers often beyond the human scale, we can no more expect to understand its thoughts and dreams than a Monarch butterfly can understand ours . . . In contemplating the future of mind in the universe, we have exhausted the resources of our puny human science.[109]

Jesus also inspires us: "I come not to destroy the law or the prophets, but to fulfill them. . . . *That you might be filled with all the fullness of God*"—that you might experience great happiness within yourself through heightened awareness, expansion of human consciousness, and highly productive work.

And when this happens, your heart will feel as if it is going to *explode* with joy. Every cell in your body will sing with joy. EVERYTHING you see, EVERYONE you meet, EVERYTHING you do at home, at work, on the street, will be touching your heart with joy. You will wake up in joy. You will go to bed with the same joy.

Krishna, the most revered Indian Avatar, declares:

To but One Goal are marching everywhere, all human beings, though they may seem to walk on paths divergent; that goal is I.[110]

The goal is to find the *Christ* (Buddha, Tao, Creator, *Joy*—that's the test) within yourself. For "Christ is everything in all of you" (Col. 3:11), attests the Bible.

In the *Cidade Caleixnese* manuscript (the so-called *Dialogue of Jesus and John*) we find another insight:

The kingdom of heaven is within you,
and whosoever shall know himself shall find it . . .
strive therefore to know yourself
and you shall know that you are in the City of God,
and you are the City.[111]

CARE:
MAKE TODAY
COUNT

Truly, we are the City of God! But we must dig deep down into ourselves to find it. Mahatma Gandhi, Dag Hammarskjold, Martin Luther King, U Thant, Werner Heisenberg, Max Planck, Carl Friedrich von Weizsäcker and a universe of other great pathfinders are witnesses to our possibility. Their lives are a challenge to us. They call out to each of us to know our truth. Reach our maximum performance. Extend our happiness through self-discipline and clear judgment.

Keep the *fire* of your love ever burning. Seek the extraordinary in your ordinary world. Tune your mind, body, and soul to become a better instrument for excellence and righteousness! *Let your higher self be your guide to fuller ways of living. Create a richer quality of life.* Make the world's problems your problems. Make today count. Care. Be the best you are capable of being. Learn to use your abilities to the fullest. Let the splendor of the Godhead be *your* splendor!

An Albanian woman, Agnes Gonxha Bojaxhiu, known to all of us as Mother Teresa of Calcutta, recipient of the Nobel Peace Prize in 1979 for her exceptional life of love. Her work replaced human abortion with human adoption. She has cared for hundreds of thousands of sick people. It is said she has treated 186,000 victims of leprosy and 22,000 dying destitutes. She has fed 126,000 hungry and homeless people in seventy-one countries. She states, "The poor *are* our Lord!"[112] "In serving the poorest we directly serve God."[113]

Mother Teresa's life reflects the words of Jesus:

> For when I was hungry you gave me something to eat, I was thirsty and you gave me something to drink, I was a stranger and you invited me in, I needed clothes and you clothed me, I was ill and you looked after me, I was in prison and you visited me. I assure you, as often as you did for one of my least brothers, you did for me (Matt. 25:35 and 40).

Furthermore:

> I tell you the truth, whatever you did not do for one of the least of these, you did not do for me (Matt. 25:45).

For we are *one and the same Being.* Yes, I am in my Father, and you [are] in me, and I [am] in you (John 14:20).

Compassion is the highest form of thought. It is pure, mindful action. "Nature gave men two ends," says George Kirkpatrick, "one to sit on and one to think with. Ever since then, man's success or failure has been dependent on the one he used most." The emptying of the lower mind precedes its being filled with the fullness of Love in its higher state.

"Wash your hearts with your tears of joy so that God might install himself therein," sings the twentieth-century Bangalore Saint, Sri Satya Sai Baba. "You have the lamp within you. Light it and march on without fear." And the Ancient One, as some called Meher Baba, elaborates:

> *The God-realized knows himself to be God as surely as a man knows himself to be a man.* It is for him not a matter of doubt, belief, self-delusion, or guess-work; *it is a supreme and unshakeable uncertainty which needs no external corroboration and remains unaffected by contradiction, because it is based upon self-knowledge.* Such spiritual certainty is incapable of being challenged. A man thinks himself to

be what in reality he is not; a God-realized knows what in reality he is.[114]

Join the gathering. For where two or three are gathered in God's name, God is in the midst of them. Be an intelligent investor in *your* life. Become a witness to classic values. Allow the windows of your consciousness to remain open. The gifts of authentic happiness and profit that will result are endless. Become the Christ, the Logos, and you will carry thoughts of joy and love.

In his letter to the Colossians, Saint Paul recommends:

Put aside your old self with its past deeds and put on a new man, one who grows in knowledge as he is *formed anew in the image of his Creator.* There is no Greek or Jew here, circumcised or uncircumcised, foreigner, Scythian, slave, or freeman. Rather, Christ is everything in all of you (Col. 3:9–11).

And what you are to become is the success you already are. "The seed of God is in you," reveals the remarkable pen of Eckhart:

Given an intelligent, hard-working farmer, it will thrive and grow up to God, whose seed it is; and according to its fruits will be God-nature. Pear seeds grow into pear trees, nut seeds into nut trees, and God seeds into God.[115]

The seven systems of Indian philosophy (Buddhism, Mimamsa, Nyaya, Sankhya, Vaisheshika, Vedanta, and Yoga) arrive at similar time-tested conclusions.

To be relaxed, we have to relax. To experience and embrace, we have to embrace. You can't swim in the ocean while you are standing on the shore. "That is why we can attain to the unitive knowledge of God," writes Huxley, "only when we become in some measure Godlike, only when we permit God's kingdom to come by making our own kingdom go."[116]

An article on "Shakespeare and Religion," written during Huxley's last weeks, contains perhaps his simplest and yet most profound statement about life and happiness:

The world is an illusion, but it is an illusion which we must take seriously, because it is real as far as it goes, and in those aspects of the reality which we are capable of apprehending. Our business is to wake up. We have to find ways in which to detect the whole of reality in the one illusory part which our self-centered consciousness permits us to see. We must not live thoughtlessly, taking our illusion for the complete reality, but at the same time we must not live too thoughtfully in the sense of trying to escape from the dream state. We must continually be on our watch for ways in which we may enlarge our consciousness. We must not attempt to live outside the world, which is given to us, but we must somehow learn how to transform it and transfigure it. Too much "wisdom" is as bad as too little wisdom, and there must be no magic tricks. We must learn to come to reality without the enchanter's wand and his book of words. One must find a way of being in the world while not being of it. A way of living in time without being completely swallowed in time.[117]

"It is through discrimination and renunciation that man understands who he really is," says Sai Baba.

The Second Vatican Council goes to the core of truth:

All men are called to one and the same goal, namely God himself.[118]

Subramuniya, who realized his true identity, joyfully sings:

When you unfold spiritually on the path, you discover what it is that you know, although you cannot easily explain it. At first you feel light shining within you. You may think it is only an illusion, yet you will find as you move into a quiet area of your mind you can see the light again and again. It becomes brighter and brighter. You will begin to wonder what is in the center of the light. . . .

As you release desires and cravings through daily meditation, the external mind releases its hold on your awareness and you dive deeper, fearlessly, into the center of this blazing avalanche of light beyond form and formlessness. And as you come back into the mind, you see the mind for what it is, and you see the mind for what it is not. . . . As you come out of that Samadhi, you realize you are the spirit, the life force of all. You become the spirit consciously, if you could say spirit has consciousness. You are that spirit in every living soul.[119]

"After the attainment of God-realization," says Meher Baba,

> *The soul discovers that it has always been the Infinite Reality, and that its looking upon itself as finite during the period of evolution and spiritual advancement was an illusion.* The soul also finds that the infinite knowledge and bliss that it enjoys have been latent in the Infinite Reality from the beginning of time and that they became manifest at the moment of realization. . . .
>
> The process of attaining God-realization is a game in which the beginning and the end are identical. The attainment of realization is nevertheless a distinct gain. There are two kinds of advantages. One consists in getting what we did not previously possess; the other consists in realizing what we really are. God-realization is of the second kind. However, there is an infinite difference in the soul that has God-realization and one that does not have it. Though the soul that has God-realization has nothing it did not already possess, its explicit knowledge makes God-realization of the highest significance. The soul that is not God-realized experiences itself as finite and is constantly troubled by the opposites of joy and sorrow. But the soul that has realization is lifted out of them and experiences the Infinite.[120]

Once you realize you are the life-force of all, you will start walking consciously in the happiness of joy. Every moment will be your moment. You will drink your life. You will drink joy's love. You will lose yourself in joy. You will understand, as I did, that *truly YOU are the visible part of the Creator, son of the Trinity — the triumphant Light Manifest:*

> *When the blazing avalanche of light*
> *and power are emanating out of your hands;*

When the head spinning love and happiness are
*   exploding out of your heart;*
And when gentle shimmering peace and joy
*   permeate every cell of your body;*
You'll understand that there is only God—the
*   I Am Who I Am;*
That it is the splendor of your own Soul that pervades
*   the entire universe;*
That you are looking at yourself through your brother's
*   eyes.*
And that the Creator of everything that is and
*   everything that you experience,*
Is really you, yourself.
There will be Joy!

Six centuries before Darwin's theory of organic evolution excited some philosophical scientists about their ancestry and evolution, Jalaluddin Rumi, in his *Masnavi,* considered by Iranians to rank in importance with the Koran itself, exultantly observed the chronology of his unfoldment to David Bohm's "plenum, which is the ground for the existence of everything . . . and into which they [everything] must ultimately vanish." In Rumi's words, "To Him [the Zero State—Non-Existence] shall we return":

I died as a mineral and became a plant.
I died as a plant and rose as an animal.
I died as an animal and I was a man.
Why then should I fear?
When was I less by dying?
Yet once more I shall die as man,
To soar with the blessed angels;
But even from angelhood I must pass on.
All except God perishes.
When I have sacrificed my angel soul,
I shall become what passes the conception of man!
Let me then become Non-Existent [the Zero

State prior to the Big Bang],
For Non-Existence sings,
"To Him shall we return."[121]

OUR ACTIONS PROPEL US THROUGH MULTI-DIMENSIONAL WORLDS

To illustrate the functioning of manifestation—that which we see and experience, we can view Godhead (*physical law,* the invariable Zero State) as an Ocean and the manifestations as "waves" (*physical quantities* —unique patterns and dimensions of the very same ocean). As will be seen later, the rate at which the waves are transferred determines the specific characteristics of each multi-dimensional pattern.

Furthermore, each pattern (physical quantity—natural unit of measurement) can be affected by other patterns. They can be added to and subtracted from the original measurement. Observe that *everything* we do every second of our life creates spacetime patterns that are added and subtracted in direct relationship to our actions, making us into a sort of tuning circuit (similar to a radio or TV tuner) *that attracts the same field it generates.*

We can verify this with the Grotthus-Draper law: *For light to produce an effect upon matter, it must be absorbed.*[122] Atoms, molecules, and cells absorb energy and become excited only when they can accept photons whose energy equals the energy difference of the levels in question; that is, the photon energy must equal exactly the energy needed to raise the configuration from one level to another. Thus, only energy of a specific frequency will be absorbed.

Absorption will continue as long as there is less energy in the lower energy level than in the higher. Similarly, if our actions have not created the proper absorption condition, we cannot participate in the effect. Because the physical law (the *Zero State*) controls mathematics as the stabilizing equilibrium (making certain that every action produces an equal and opposite reaction), all pleasant or unpleasant experiences are therefore only the *consequences* of our own actions. They would not be there had we not created them. *If the necessary electromagnetic field did not exist within us, there would be no way for the experience to "tune in."* Although there are thousands of radio and television programs being broadcast, we only see and hear those we "tune in" to.

Suppose we create abundance, joy, and happiness for someone. Consider the mathematics: what we did involved the multidimensional quantities of time, space, and energy. The force intensity of our action set appropriate physical law measurements in motion. We can't escape them. *The action produced must be counterbalanced.* In the future, we will not only have to understand the functioning of the Zero State equilibrium, but in order to *know the truth* and achieve a higher degree of freedom, human closeness, abundance, and joy, we will also have to act accordingly. A new being will then be born. A new glory and Great Light will be manifest upon the earth.

This rebirth (not a return to the mother's womb and rebirth therefrom, but a metaphorical rebirth of interior illumination into higher consciousness and awareness) is alluded to by Christ in his dialogue with Nicodemus when he says, "Do not be surprised because I tell you, 'You must be born again'" (John 3:7 GN). The Hindus have a similar term, "twice-born," which refers to interior rebirth and the illumination that culminates with the widening of our spine's central channel for greater production, release, and conscious control of very large amounts of our life-force (bioplasma), the fuel for greater productivity, happiness, and fulfillment.

This is the goal of our liberation: to achieve a new order of human society, to progress towards higher knowledge and cosmic sense; to live in a world of light, splendor, peace, and goodness, more breathtaking and more beautiful than anything our intellects can imagine now.

87

YOUR FUTURE
IS VERY
BRIGHT

In his letter to the Romans, Saint Paul attests to the quantum breakthrough:

> *Indeed, the whole created world eagerly awaits the revelation of the sons of God...* because the world itself will be *freed from its slavery...* and share in the glorious [peace and] freedom of the children of God (Rom. 8:19, 21).

"Just as a river," confirms Swami Muktananda,

> After flowing for a long time, merges in the ocean and becomes the ocean, when Kundalini [the seed of pure pleasure] has finished Her work and stabilized in the sahasrara, you become completely immersed in God. All your impurities and coverings are destroyed, and you take complete rest in the Self. The veil which made you see duality drops away, and you experience the world as a blissful play of Kundalini, a sport of God's energy. You see the universe as supremely blissful light, undifferentiated from yourself, and you remain unshakeable in this awareness. This is the state of liberation, the state of perfection.

A being who has attained this state does not have to close his eyes and retire to a solitary place to get into *samadhi*. [Note, *samadhi* is a state of complete peace (stillness) of the mind, heart, and soul. Christian mystics refer to it as *union* (unitive life) with God, and Buddhists as *nirvana*. In this spiritual union,[123] the bioplasma energy *continually* (day and night) flows, in large quantities through you. You drink—as if you had an uninterrupted sexual orgasm—a "wine of pure pleasure."] Whether he is meditating, eating, bathing, sleeping, whether he is alone or with others, he experiences the peace and joy of the Self. Whatever he sees is God, whatever he hears is God, whatever he tastes is God, whatever words he speaks are God's. In the midst of the world, he experiences the solitude of a cave, and in the midst of people, he experiences the bliss of samadhi . . . the bliss of the world is the *ecstasy* of *samadhi*.

It is to attain this that we should meditate, that we should have our Kundalini awakened. We do not meditate to attain God, because we have already attained Him. We meditate so that we can become aware of God manifest within us . . .

And this is why I always tell everyone, "Meditate on your Self, honor your Self, worship your Self, for God dwells within you as you."[124]

Yes, "Father," the man of Galilee petitioned:

I pray . . . that all may be one as you, Father, are in me, and I in you; I pray that they may be in us . . . I living in them, you living in me—that their unity [understanding and knowledge] may be complete (John 17:20–21, 23).

And when this happens, we will, like Bohm, Sheldrake, Wald, Prigogine, Weizsäcker and other philosophical scientists, validate that there is but One body and One mind. You and everyone else are luminous cells of that One living body of God (Eph. 4:4, 1 Cor. 10:17, Gal. 3:28). One living heart. One glory and One joy. One eternal You.

The Jesuit philosopher and paleontologist Teilhard de Chardin brilliantly presents a fascinating and wonderful story—one of mystery, awe, beauty, and inspiration in his *Future of Man:*

> The Incarnation is a making new, a restoration, of *all* the universe's forces and powers; Christ is the instrument, the Center, the End, of the *whole* of animate and material creation: through Him, *everything* is created, sanctified, and vivified. This is the constant and general teaching of Saint John and Saint Paul [that most "cosmic" of sacred writers], and it has passed into the most solemn formulas of the Liturgy; and yet we repeat it, and generations to come will go on repeating it, without ever being able to grasp or appreciate the *profound* and mysterious significance, bound up as it is with understanding of the universe.[125]

He adds triumphantly:

> The men of the future will form, in some way, but one single consciousness; and since, once their initiation is complete, they will have gauged the strength of their associated minds, the immensity of the universe, and the straitness of their prison, this consciousness will be truly adult and of age . . . It is then, we may be sure, that the Parousia will be realized in creation that has been taken to the climax of its capacity for union. The single act of assimilation and synthesis that has been going on since the beginning of time will then at last be made plain, and the universal Christ will blaze out like a flash of lightning in the storm clouds of a world whose slow consecration is complete.[126]

The astrophysicist John A. Wheeler, further elaborates:

> The universe not only must give rise to life, but . . . once life is created, it will endure forever, become infinitely knowledgeable, and *ultimately mold the universe to its will* . . . thus man—or Life— will be not only the measure of all things, but their creator as well.[127]

REJOICE, FOR
YOU ARE
JOY

It will be seen in the Unified Quantities Theory that all creation manifests different aspects of the same reality (there is *hierarchical relationship* between matter, energy, charge, electric and magnetic flux density, time, force, motion, electric and magnetic fields, and so on), and once we encounter Godhead in man (Gautama the Buddha in *The Lotus Sutra* says: "I am the Father. All living things are my children.") And Christ restates: "Whoever has seen me has seen the Father" (John 14:9). We encounter the Creator (the same essence) in all things!

As physics and mathematics show, if Invariance (the ocean—that-which-is, the physical law) IS UNITED TO ALL POINTS (we hear often "God is everywhere"), THEN ALL POINTS ARE UNITED THROUGH INVARIANCE TO THEMSELVES. Listen to the immortal message: "I am in my Father, and you in me, and I in you" (John 14:20).

Chinese, Indian, American, Japanese, Russian, German, Ukrainian, Swede, Arab, French, English, Spanish, Italian, white, black, yellow, the man you help or hurt, is no one else but YOURSELF. Jesus knew this, as did Schroedinger, Eddington, Planck, Heisenberg, Bohm, Ruysbroeck, Suso, Huang Po, Kabir, William Law, Dag Hammarskjold, and many others.[128] They all perceived that *the same essence is not only without, but also within* [the observer and the observed are fundamentally one]. And I MYSELF AM PART OF THE SAME LIVING ESSENCE.

A moment of such belonging was recounted to me by a friend:

> It was summer vacation for students. I was walking the deserted grounds of the college campus and thinking: "God show me how I can love you more and more." As I approached a large willow tree its branches all of a sudden started coming towards me, seemingly magnetized, touching me with a tremendous feeling of love. I extended my hands as if asking for a gift. Next, I felt a burning sensation in the palms of my hands and a great power coming upon me. (The heat and blisters, in the palms of my hands, stayed with me for several days.) I lost the feeling of my body. The willow tree dissolved before me, transforming itself into a great skyscraper, like one of the twin towers of the World Trade Center. As I looked up at the building, each floor became infused with a unique dimension and reality. Each one became a distinct level of God that was vibrating like a TV channel at different frequencies. I stood there transfixed. The experience lasted for no more than an hour. But in that time I learned that what is revealed in our visible universe of galaxies and stars is nothing compared to what is hidden. For as I had looked up, I had found that the building was floor upon floor, reality upon reality, universe upon universe of innumerable worlds of brilliant light, beauty and color. There was no top to the building, only a moment of disappearance as it leapt beyond my sight into the higher worlds of boundless consciousness and joy. Then I understood that I must attain mastery over higher faculties of love and *feeling* before I can move more freely to the higher dimensions of God.

The keen understanding that we are the Light of Life is one that is corroborated by other cultures and has been referred to by Christians as Christ formed within you; Pan-Asians know it as becoming a Buddha (Awakened or Enlightened One);[129] Sri Aurobindo described it as evolving to the Mind of Light;[130] the Swami Rama understands it as reaching the state of Superconsciousness or Absolute Samadhi;[131] and the Canadian psychiatrist Maurice Bucke calls it Cosmic Consciousness.[132]

Let us look at other men and women who have achieved this understanding. Moses did not just break into light and happiness. It took a lot of "mountain climbing" (fasting from undesirable habits— purification) before he reached the top (illumination) of Mount Sinai.[133] But once he did, he must have *trembled* in joy when he saw the Truth. Oh, what happiness—what glory . . . "I AM WHO I AM"—*I am the very same essence in different states and forms* —was understood.

Jesus, the Greatest Living Light, also had to *undergo inner growth and overcome obstacles* (John 16:33). He learned to obey through suffering (Heb. 5:8) and endless testing (Mark 1:13). He was "tempted in every way that we are" (Heb. 4:15); and prayed, "Abba [Oh Father] . . . take this cup away from me. But let it be as you would have it, not as I" (Mark 14:36).

Jesus, says Maurice Nicol, in his interpretation of some parables and miracles of Christ, *The New Man,* "had to pass through all the stages of this evolution *in himself* by trial and error, until it was perfected, through endless inner temptations, of which we are only given a few glimpses."[134]

Had he not, we could have questioned the whole development process of a young Creator, for not having to face the same hardships we do. Yet in the earliest reference to the Son of Man's growth, it is said, "Jesus, for His part, *progressed steadily* in wisdom and age and grace before God and men" (Luke 2:52).

"Like a seed in the beginning," writes John Haughey in *The Conspiracy of God:*

> [he] progressed from there to seedling, to plant, to tree, to glorious fulfillment. . . . And at some point in his life, he knew something that only the Spirit could eventually teach men when time had provided a sufficient cushion for them to accept what must have made Jesus *gasp* when he saw the truth.[135]

When he understood that he is the Creator himself—when he had enough courage to say, "Whoever has seen me has seen the Father" (John 14:9)—*whoever has seen the wave has seen the Ocean* —he became the Light, the Path, and the Happiness for others. "I am the way" to freedom, he said concisely, "No one comes to the Father but through me" (John 14:6)—through letting go the undesirable baggage of self-oppression—through a Christ life of love, purity of heart, detachment, stillness, and happiness.

The kingdom is not a place you go to, he enumerates on various occasions. It is a mode of living, being, rejoicing, and loving. It is a state of existence. But to understand what Jesus is saying, we have to apply his words, we have to attain mastery over higher faculties of consciousness:

> Reform your lives! (Matt. 4:17) You must be made perfect as your heavenly Father is perfect (Matt. 5:48).

"Remove the rust of wrong ideas,"[136] recommends Milarepa, "root up all errors from within!" . . . Wherever you go, whatever you do, help people to feel at ease, spread happiness and a sense of well-being. Live a life of love in action. *The more you love, the more you will understand—the more your effectiveness will increase.* There will be Joy. There will be Light Triumphant manifest in your being.

The Galilean advises us to love God with all of our heart, and all our mind and all of our power; and to love our neighbor as ourselves. Remember, God is everywhere, including in your neighbor. We should, therefore, *love* everything, including our neighbor, *for he and she are we!* Then we will experience peace. Then we will experience love. Then we will experience joy that surpasses all understanding.

Our mission will be accomplished. There will be a jail break! Our chains will fall away. We shall be set FREE! Free from what? From the Disneyland spacetime movie that we have entertained ourselves with. "For I am the first and the last," shares Carey:

> The beginning and the end, the Creator of all that is and of all that is to be. My potential is infinite, my Being eternal. All creation is an ever-unfolding picture of what I conceive. The star fields are my canvas, humans are my brushes, biology is my paint.[137]

"It is only by becoming Godlike that we can know God," writes Aldous Huxley:

—And to become Godlike is to identify ourselves with the divine element which in fact constitutes *our* essential nature, but of which, in our mainly voluntary ignorance, we choose to remain unaware.[138]

Albert Schweitzer, Martin Buber, H. G. Wells, Thomas Merton, Rabindranath Tagore, Pablo Casals, and a growing universe of others in all climes and cultures give us a similar story. The great Fathers of the Church: Irenaeus, Clement of Alexandria, Gregory of Nyssa, Cyril of Alexandria, Augustine, and particularly Basil the Great[139], all understood that each person slowly progresses through stages of awakening and gradually becomes perfected in the image and likeness of his or her Creator. Let us listen to Basil the Great describe the stages of awakening and transformation into God:

> Through His aid, hearts are lifted up, the weak are led by the hand, and they who are advancing are brought to perfection. By His illumination of those who are purified from all defilement, He makes them spiritual by fellowship with Him. Just as bright and transparent bodies, in contact with a ray of light, themselves become translucent, and emit a fresh radiance from themselves, so souls wherein the Divine Spirit dwells, being illuminated thereby, themselves become spiritual and give forth their grace to others. Hence comes their foreknowledge of the future, the understanding of mysteries, the comprehension of what is hidden, the distribution of good gifts, the heavenly citizenship, a place in the choir of angels.
>
> Hence comes to them unending joy, abiding in God, being made like unto God, and which is the highest of all, *being made God.*[140]

Saint Paul rejoices in his art of living:

> *The life I live now is not my own;*
> *Christ is living in me* (Gal. 2:20).

"Or perhaps it might be more accurate to use the verb transitively and say," recommends Aldous Huxley, "I live, yet not; for it is the logos

(Creator) who *lives in me* —lives in me as an actor lives his part."[141]
 And Saint Catherine of Genoa exclaims in happy wonder:

My Me is God, nor do I recognize any other Me except my God himself.[142]

Jalaluddin Rumi of Afghanistan says in the same words as the Blessed Angela of Foligno:

I am you and you are me.[143]

The Upanishads sing joyfully:

I am the Infinite;
What you are, that same am I;
You are all This;
I am all This.[144]

Mechthild of Magdeburg develops the same kind of singular eloquence:

I am in you and you are in me.
We cannot be closer.
We are two united, poured into a single form by an eternal fusion.[145]

Among many quotations from the mystics of the Mohammedan faith, this Sufi sets more music to rhyme:

There's naught within your robe but God Himself
The knower and the known are but the same.
He who knows God is God;
God knows Him-Self.[146]

Saint Augustine shares with us:

Lord, I have sought you in all the temples of the world and lo, *I found you within myself....* If a man does not find the Lord within himself, he will surely not find Him in the world.[147]

IS
ANYBODY
HERE EXCEPT
GOD?

Long before Buddha, Ashtavakra cried out, "Aho Aham! Namo Mahyam!" Afterwards, Bayazid of Bistun re-echoed him: "How wonderful am I! Salutations unto Me! How great is my glory!: On another occasion someone knocked at this Sufi saint's door and cried, "Is Bayazid here?" Bayazid answered, "Is anybody here except God?"[148]

"The heavens are mine," rejoices Saint John of the Cross:

> The earth is mine, and the nations are mine!
> Mine are the just, and the sinners are mine;
> Mine are the angels and the Mother of God;
> All things are mine.
> God himself is mine and for me,
> Because Christ is mine and all for me.
> What do you ask for,
> What do you seek for, O my soul?
> All is yours—all is for you.
> Do not take less nor rest with the crumbs
> Which fall from the table of your Father.
> Go forth and exult in your glory,

Hide yourself in it, and rejoice,
And you shall obtain all desires of your heart.[149]

When Pope Paul VI expressed this beautiful song, his heart must have embraced in happiness not only all of humanity, but the whole universe:

Let us rejoice and give thanks that we have become not only Christians but Christ. My brothers, do you understand the grace of God our Head? Stand in admiration, rejoice; we have become Christ.[150]

This Sufi saint, in perfect harmony with a thousand others[151], exclaims gratefully in joy and happiness:

I saw You not before—I see You now,
Belov'd! You peep forth from every face!
I saw You not before—behind the clouds
Beloved! You did not hide. I see you now![152]

And

As loving man and wife, when they embrace,
Are both dissolved in but one feel of Love,
One feel of Unity, and know naught else
Outside their body or inside their mind;
E'en more, the Soul when it embraces God,
And feels its Unity with the All-Self,
Passes beyond all sorrow, all desire;
For all desire is now fulfilled.[153]

PART II:

VERIFICATIONS:
ALL
IS ONE
ESSENCE

QUANTITIES:
THE
KEY TO
THE UNIVERSE

Let us consider the most sacred frontier of physics and mathematics. Can the Ultimate Reality, the Invariance, the Unmoved Mover itself, be verified?

Yes! Here, in the domain of mathematical concepts and formulations, in a world filled with high-energy particle accelerators, thermonuclear fusion, physical constant measurement theory, thermodynamics, radioactivity, relativity, quantum physics, superstrings, and beyond, the Ultimate Reality (Godhead) is actually very carefully measured, analyzed, and categorized through what physics commonly refers to as physical quantities and physical laws.

In truth, physics is a science that deals with the ultimate makeup of nature. *Physics measures the NATURE of Invariance.* For every basic building block, or physical quantity, of nature has a fixed relationship to every other one. They are all truly INVARIABLE—unchangeable—unmovable. In this sense *Physics measures the nature of God!*

It is difficult to believe that the *rigorously* scientific methods of physics have been with us for only 320 years. Within that time tremendous progress has been made in physics by *unifying* the rich complexity of assorted physical phenomena *through simple physical quantities.*

This incredible chapter in human history has been written on the crowded canvas of time by such great scientists as Newton, Coulomb, Ampere, Oersted, Gauss, Faraday, Maxwell, De Broglie, Eddington, Rutherford, Einstein, Bohr, Jeans, Born, Steinmetz, Schroedinger, Planck, Pauli, Heisenberg, Bohm, Jordan, Weizsäcker, Atkins, Weinberg, Salam, Glashow, Hawking, Silk, Dürr, Witten, and other creative geniuses. They have elegantly summarized the myriad forms of nature into the mathematical equivalents of the physical quantities of time, space, matter. These physical quantities, which are the *natural units of measurement,* and their universal ratios we call physical laws.

Freeman Dyson, who takes a worm's eye view of this odd universe, states in his beautiful book *Infinite in All Directions:*

> Now it is generally true that the very greatest scientists in each discipline are unifiers. This is especially true in physics. Newton and Einstein were supreme as unifiers. The great triumphs of physics have been triumphs of unification. We almost take it for granted that the road of progress in physics will be a wider and wider unification, bringing more and more phenomena within the scope of a few fundamental principles. Einstein was so confident of the correctness of this road of unification that at the end of his life he took almost no interest in the experimental discoveries which were then beginning to make the world of physics more complicated. It is difficult to find among physicists any serious voices in opposition to unification.[154]

Through testing, experimentation, and sophisticated instrumentation, we are on the verge of moving from a state of descriptive insight and speculation (which save for a few mystics has been the sacred cow of world thought for centuries) to a discipline that is supported with proper tools of scientific investigation, hypothesis, and testing.

We are on the verge, through physics and mathematics, of realizing mankind's age-old dream of a unified understanding of the universe and of Who we are, What we are, Why we are, and What kind of world this is.

"There has been a transformation, during the past decade, in our understanding of the inanimate physical universe—a 'quantum jump,'" states the Nobel Laureate in Physics, Abdus Salam, "that lies primarily in the understanding of the nature of the four forces and a comprehension of the earliest history of the universe."

"Everybody likes adventure stories," says Paul Davis in his *Superforce:*

> One of the greatest adventures of all time is happening now, in the shadowy world of fundamental physics. The characters in the story are scientists and their quest is for a prize of unimaginable value—nothing less than the key to the universe. The most important scientific discovery of our age is that *the physical universe did not always exist.* Science faces no greater challenge than to explain how the universe came to exist and why it is structured in the way it is. I believe that in the last few years that challenge has been met. For the first time in history we have a rational scientific theory of all existence. This revolutionary breakthrough represents an advance of unparalleled magnitude in our understanding of the world and will have profound repercussions for man's conception of the cosmos and his place within it.[155]

Such a discovery of finding one's place was told to me by a friend:

> I was baffled by zero. And I contemplated it. I came into a great hall. And there I realized that zero was nowhere and everywhere. It was the imperceptible substratum of *nothingness* from which all matter was created. It was an *arbitrary* point. It could be anywhere, any place in the hall where we begin counting. Furthermore, zero contains within itself a + and a − polarity which are opposite and electrically complementary to each other, dependent on the direction of counting one takes.

The mathematical ideas of physics go back to ancient Sumeria, Mesopotamia, and Egypt. Man kept a record of what he owned. The agents of government measured the land and its known goods while the priests and philosophers reflected on the general nature of the mysterious, unfathomable forces.

The legendary stories from the history of science are helpful. The Greek Archimedes, a genius in both mathematics and physical insight, was once asked by King Hieron II of Syracuse to find out whether a goldsmith had substituted less valuable silver for gold in making the king's new crown. While getting into a bathtub, Archimedes realized that anything put into the tub of water would displace its own volume of water. He instantly leaped out of his bath and ran naked through the streets to King Hieron's palace shouting "Eureka! Eureka!" ("I have found the answer, I have found the answer!").

This earlier wild frontier of mathematical physics began to be somewhat tamed, systematized, and unified. In 1665 the twenty-three-year-old Isaac Newton, presumably while lying in the orchard of Woolsthorpe in Lincolnshire, England, saw an apple fall to earth. This remarkable event set him to work on the problem of what caused both the apple to fall and the moon to orbit. He found that bodies attract each other with a force inversely proportional to the square of the distance between them. With this law of universal gravitation, he *brought together the quantities* of mass, force, and distance.

In addition to his first and second laws of motion, which are perhaps one of the greatest generalizations and useful theorems of natural sciences, he unified the quantities of acceleration with mass and force.

Newton's laws of gravity and motion are relatively simple mathematically, even by high school standards. Nevertheless, the scientific revolution that accompanied the work of Newton provided a classic example of how what seems to be a very involved, random behavior (and sometimes a complicated mass of events) can, using the elegant mathematical descriptions of a physical system, be revealed as simple physical *quantities* that can support a vast range of complex activities in nature. These physical quantities are encoded through mathematical relationships of physical laws in a cryptic and often subtle way, and are not always readily apparent to someone studying nature itself.

"Consider how all events are *interconnected,*" states the great mathematician-philosopher and Harvard professor of philosophy Alfred North Whitehead:

> When we see the lightning, we listen for the thunder; when we hear the wind, we look for the waves on the sea; in the chill autumn, the leaves fall. Everywhere order reigns, so that when some circumstances have been noted, we can foresee that others will also be present. The progress of science consists in observing

these *interconnections* and in showing with a patient ingenuity that the events of this ever-shifting world are but examples of a few general *connections* or *relations* called laws. To see what is general in what is particular and what is permanent in what is transitory is the aim of scientific thought. In the eye of science, the fall of an apple, the motion of a planet round a sun, and the clinging of the atmosphere to the earth are all seen as examples of the law of gravity. This possibility of disentangling the most complex evanescent circumstances into various examples of permanent laws is the controlling idea of modern thought.[156]

By integrating, through mathematical substitution, the various physical quantities in their equations, one can discover a full range of hidden connections, relationships, symmetries, and superhuman insights never suspected on physical grounds.

For example, we all know that gravity controls our lives from birth to death and with a tight grip it holds every particle, every planet, and every star together. For years mankind has been dreaming about leaving earth and visiting distant galaxies in some type of antigravity vehicle. Yet how do we enter into the heart of gravity without using great masses of hardware and miles of wiring and plumbing?

When one evaluates the mathematics of astronomical gravitation with physical quantities, one notices that Newton's law of universal gravitation can be extended from the simple relationship of *force* (F) divided by *mass* (m) (y = F/m) to a more exotic expression, where *gravity* (y) equals *linear velocity* (v) times *angular velocity* (T) (y = vT). (For linear velocity and angular velocity equations, please refer to Table 2 in Appendix B.) By studying the equations of angular velocity more closely, one can further deduce that to change the angular velocity of an interstellar vehicle (particle) one could apply a magnetic field to matter and thus modify the radius of each particle to produce an anti-gravity technology. Hence, from what one sees on the surface as a challenge, through physical quantities, one can discover a full range of new possibilities.

From approximately 1780 to 1789, Coulomb, a Frenchman, found that magnetic poles attract or repel each other in proportion to the inverse square of their distances. He also discovered that the same law holds for electric charges. Coulomb's Law, which appears very similar to Newton's law of universal gravitation, *unified the quantities* of force, charge, and distance.

The Dane Oersted's discovery in 1820 that electric currents exert a force on magnets paved the way for France's Ampere to formulate the mathematical law of force as well as to show that the quantities of electric currents exert force upon each other.

Michael Faraday in 1831–32, through the momentous laws of induction between currents and between currents and magnets, showed that magnetism and electricity were also closely *related,* each feeding off the other. He discovered the phenomenon of electromagnetic induction— the production of electric current by a change of magnetic intensity.

In 1873, the great mathematical physicist, James Clerk Maxwell, achieved a tremendous breakthrough with his electromagnetic theory. Building upon Faraday's work, he showed with a system of equations that electricity and magnetism are intimately *related* forces that can be described by a unified electromagnetic field. Maxwell *united the quantities* of electrical and magnetic fields, force, velocity, distance, and charge. He showed, with mathematical elegance, that what at first sight could appear as two distinct forces of nature are, in fact, just *two different facets of the same single force.* The stunning success of Maxwell's and Faraday's *unification* can be measured by the tremendous impact that electrical power and electronics—which come from the electromagnetic field concept—have had on our lives.

In 1888, Hertz, a German, building on Maxwell's work, produced electric vibrations by direct electrical method. His experiments laid the groundwork for our present wireless communication.

Albert Einstein, whose life, in fact, to use his own words, was "divided between politics and equations," boldly interpreted physical quantities to prove that *the quantities of energy and mass are also the same essence, the same thing* but in different forms. Furthermore, he demonstrated, following Henri Poincare and Heinrich Lorentz's mathematical operations, that *the quantities of space and time* are not independent entities, but are *interwoven.* He took the subtle "rotations" of Lorentz-Poincare symmetry peculiar effect, so contrary to common sense, and with elegant mathematical manipulations of physical quantities, gave birth to the new physics that rocked the scientific community and changed the face of the twentieth century.

His next quest, to *link* all natural phenomena into a single descriptive scheme, proved a little bit more elusive. Einstein's lifelong quest to construct a complete, unified theory of everything in the universe, all at one go, could probably have been realized, had he had a little more time.

Davis states:

For the first time in history we have within our grasp a complete scientific theory of the whole universe in which no physical object or system lies outside a small set of basic scientific principles. . . . These dramatic developments stem directly from a number of major advances made in fundamental physics over the last decade, especially in the area known as high-energy in theoretical understanding are, if anything, even more spectacular. Two new conceptual schemes are currently forcing the pace. One goes under the name of "grand unified theories," or GUTS, the other is called "supersymmetry." Together these investigations point towards a compelling idea, that all nature is ultimately controlled by the activities of a single superforce. The superforce would have the power to bring the universe into being and to furnish it with light, energy, matter, and structure. It would represent an amalgamation of matter, spacetime, and force into an integrated and harmonious framework that bestows upon the universe a hitherto UNSUSPECTED UNITY.[157]

INVARIANCE:
THE FUNDAMENTAL
ESSENCE

At the present time physics accepts the unity of the universe. The central issue is only that of the nature of its interconnectedness. Some conceptual schemes of grand unified theories are focused primarily on the unification of electromagnetism, gravity, and the strong and weak forces; others on string theories, supergravity theories, and so forth; still others claim there is no ultimate theory of the universe.

While the search goes on for a "wider and wider unification" of physics and related topics, [158] we have taken the liberty of bringing the challenge into sharper focus by *further weaving together the forgotten physical quantities* of nature and thus showing, through the *common links of invariance,* the unity of nature and how the Unmovable Mover and Creator of all "takes a seat" in the moving affairs of men.

To permit this greater depth and inclusion of contemporary material into the vital issue of who we are, and where we have come from, let us start at the beginning: What exactly is a physical quantity?

David Halliday, professor of physics at the University of Pittsburgh, and Robert Resnick, professor of physics at the Renesselaer Polytechnic Institute, write in their book *Physics for Students of Science and Engineering:*

The *building blocks* of physics are the *physical quantities* in terms of which the laws of physics are expressed. Among these are force, time, velocity, density, temperature, charge, magnetic susceptibility, and numerous others.[159]

Moreover, according to Halliday and Resnick, and we know this to be true from Einstein's Theory of Relativity:

All physical laws are the same in all reference frames. Observers in different frames [of reference] may obtain different numerical values for measured physical quantities, but the relationship between the measured quantities, that is, the laws of physics, will be the same for all observers.[160]

Earlier, in the Adam and Eve parable, we made an attempt to decode the cryptic statements of the Genesis. Let us now evaluate, through the eyes of physics, the specifics of Halliday's and Resnick's statements.

The building blocks of physics are the physical quantities. This is true, however, physical quantities are not only fundamental building blocks of physics, but of the whole of nature. Therefore, *time, space, energy, matter, and other physical quantities are the fundamental properties of nature that physics can measure.* That is, time can be measured. You do it with your watch everyday. Velocity and length can be measured. You can do it with your speedometer, your yardstick, and so forth.

We customarily say that physical laws are expressed through relationships of physical quantities. This is true. It is similar to saying that a dime is equal to a nickel plus five pennies or that $2 = 8/4$.

However, because we have not come to grips as yet with what the fundamental essence of time or gravity is, or what the fundamental essence of matter or energy is, we use the relationships among physical quantities to describe them in terms of each other. This situation is comparable to that of the days of early trading, before money existed; we exchanged chickens for goats, cows for skins, and so forth.

Suppose you went to a distant galaxy, and there, in their halls of science, these four-foot certainty principle builders presented you with numerical relationships of $2 = 8/4$, $10 = 5 \times 2$, $7 = 14/2$, and $6 = 2 \times 3$. You are told about the Tao of mathematics:

1. It has taken them many years and much money in their laboratories to prove with their "numbertrons" that the above relationships are invariable, and hold for all reference frames. In fact, you are informed that one of their great scientists, Albert Onestone, proved that the relationship between the numbers you have in your possession, that is, the laws of numbers, will be the same no matter how fast you travel in your rocket.

2. Although they understand the relationships between the numbers, which they call "mathematical laws," they have not solved as yet the *global order* (sequence, as first, second, third, and so on) *of each number.*

3. Your mission, should you decide to accept it, is to unravel the hierarchical perspective — the numerical sequence of 2, 8, 4, 10, 5, 2, 7, 14, 2, 6, 2, 3 of each number.

Of course, you smile — you know the decimal system of numeration from planet Earth. Triumphantly you write on the board 2, 3, 4, 5, 6, 7, 8, 10, 14.

Now, what does this have to do with quantities, the unified theory of physics, and your being the Unmovable Mover and the Creator of all? I was hoping you would ask. Thank you for reminding me.

Please notice that the scientist on the distant planet and our scientist on planet Earth both concluded that the relationships between numbers and the relationships between physical quantities will always be the same — *invariable, immovable.* That is, the quantity relationship of mass to energy will always be the same; the space-to-gravity relationship will also always be the same — no matter how fast you travel on your laser beam.

Eureka! We are getting very close to the Unmovable Mover. How? Note that the basic building blocks, or physical quantities, have a fixed relationship to each other. They are *invariable — unchanged — UNMOVABLE.* Like the Unmovable Mover all of the great thinkers have been talking about.

That is, *all physical quantities measure the nature of the same fundamental essence, which is Invariance.* Something that does not change. You are there! You have arrived! You are observing the Unmovable Mover through *invariable quantities* of time, mass, energy, gravity, and so forth.

Remember Halliday and Resnick—all physical laws are the same in all reference frames no matter what unit system is chosen to express them.

To put it simply, in the universal theater, the invariable laws of physics, which have been tested and retested painstakingly over the last 320 years by scientists, prove without a shadow of doubt that the physical superstructure—*the interrelated physical quantities and the relationship among the quantities are invariable and unchangeable.*

Because *we are part of the invariable quantities, we are a part of the same essence—the same thing, but in different states and forms. We are a part of the Unmoved Mover.* We are the Creator! Recall Christ's statement, "I am in the Father, and you in me, and I in you" (John 14:20).

Note another deep truth by Albert Einstein:

A human being is a part of the whole . . . a part limited in time and space. He experiences himself, his thoughts and feelings as something separated from the rest—a kind of optical delusion of his consciousness.[161]

The human being is part of the whole. And the laws of physics attest to it. Time is connected to space. Space is connected to gravity. We are connected to them too. Because we are living in time and space, we are part of the whole—part of Invariance. "We are members of one another," as Saint Paul said.

For a very simple demonstration, please reflect on your bond with other people. Please note that the *same* space that fuses your body also fuses your family, your friends, and EVERYONE you know. If space were gone, everything else would be gone. The gravitational field you walk in, likewise, not only connects all the electrons, protons, and neutrons in your body, but also all matter in the universe and everything else that you are in contact with. If the gravitational field were gone, everything else would be gone as well. This common relatedness also holds true for time, energy, electromagnetism, and other quantity connections.

Even the "Big Bang theory implies," says Rupert Sheldrake in *Noetic Sciences Review,*

That all the particles of matter in the universe come from a common source, and are, therefore, in some sense ancestrally related. Now, if we take seriously Bell's theorem and the implications of modern physics—that things that were one time connected and then separated retain a kind of nonlocal connectedness among themselves—this would imply that everything in the universe is indeed connected. We know from the theory of gravitation, ever since Newton, that *all matter in the universe is actually connected with all other matter through the gravitational force.* We now think of it in terms of the gravitational field. So this, like all evolutionary theories, takes us back to the idea of a common origin and the ideas of our relatedness, not only to other forms of life, but indeed to the entire universe in the last analysis.[162]

THE
SAME
ESSENCE IN
DIFFERENT CONTAINERS

Now let us take a closer look, like explorers who go to a distant galaxy to unravel the numerical sequence in the decimal system of numeration, at the physical quantities. Let us see how the fundamental building blocks of nature are *globally* arranged in the grand hierarchical superstructure—let us unravel, as with numbers, the *global quantity-sequence.*

When we were children, we were taught, in our arithmetic classes, that we must always *multiply* apples *with* apples, and oranges with oranges. For the multiplication to work we were instructed *not to mix* apples with oranges.

By the time we went to high school, we learned to *bundle* apples or oranges into boxes, truckloads, and shiploads, but still *no mixing* was allowed.

These boxes, truckloads, and shipload collections of *units of measurement* did not change the apple with apple multiplication game. They enabled us, however, with *higher* level systems *to bundle together identical essence,* to establish a one-one relationship within the same essence, to more subtly speed up our counting process. Eureka—Eureka! There is our grand unification of apples with apples but only in different-sized containers—in different units of measurement.

"In seeking a definition of a number," writes Bertrand Russell in his *Introduction to Mathematical Philosophy:*

> The first thing to be clear about is what we may call the grammar of our inquiry. Many philosophers, when attempting to define number, are really setting to work to define plurality, which is quite a different thing. *Number* is what is characteristic of numbers, as *man* is what is characteristic of men ... Number is a way of *bringing together* certain collections, namely, those that have a given number of terms. We can suppose all couples in one *bundle,* all trios in another, and so on. In this way, we obtain various *bundles of collections,* each bundle consisting of all the collections that have a certain number of terms. Each bundle is a class whose members are collections, i.e., classes, thus each is a class of classes ... It is obvious to common sense that two finite classes have the same number of terms if they are similar, but not otherwise. The act of counting consists in establishing a one-one relationship between the set of objects counted and the natural numbers [excluding 0] that are used up in the process.[163]

Similarly, when we multiply the quantity of matter times the velocity of light squared and get the quantity of energy, we must remember the apple with apple example from our reading, writing, and arithmetic years. This is what Albert Einstein proved with his famous energy/mass equation, namely, that the quantity of matter and quantity of energy are interchangeable—they are the very same essence PACKAGED IN DIFFERENT CONTAINERS. Maxwell did a similar apples—with—apples deduction. He proved, as previously noted, that the physical quantities of magnetism and electricity are also different aspects of the same thing.

Note, *IT WOULD BE IMPOSSIBLE TO DO ANY KIND OF PHYSICAL QUANTITY MULTIPLICATION IF THE CENTER CORE CONTENT—THE ESSENCE WE WERE MULTIPLYING —THE INVARIANCE—WERE OF AN UNRELATED CONTENT.*

What we are seeing from the mathematical formulations of physical quantities and relationships among the vast organizational linkages in this multidimensional structure of physical quantities, is that time, space, gravity, and so on, are not only fundamental building blocks of nature that physics can measure, but also *the very same fundamental essence* (*the very same reality* in different-sized containers). Simply put, because we can multiply and divide the physical quantities by each other, the quantity difference is in the measure.

A few physical quantities of time, space, energy, and velocity make an atom. Enough atoms of hydrogen, oxygen, aluminum, silicon, and iron make a brick. A few bricks make up a wall. A few walls and a roof make a house, and so forth.

Hence, the physical quantity, the atom, the brick or the wall, like numbers, "bring together certain collections, namely, those that have a given number of terms," as Bertrand Russell stated. They bring together *different container sizes* — different systems (units of measure, dimensions) of the same fundamental essence.

THE
GRAND
HIERARCHICAL
STAIRWAY

When we look beneath the surface of each element we see, as with physical quantities, a very orderly periodic system of classification. Atoms differ from one another in the number of protons and neutrons in the nucleus, and in the number of electrons spinning around the nucleus. Today the atomic number, which indicates each element's position in the table, is of fundamental significance in that it gives the number of protons possessed by the atom of the element.

Furthermore, the number of electrons, protons, neutrons, and their arrangement determine almost all the properties of the element and thus govern its position in the table.

But observe, as we go down the periodic table of elements (which was first devised by Dimitri Mendeleev, a Russian, in 1869), and keep adding a few more protons, neutrons, and electrons, the face of each element changes. Like boxes and truckloads of apples, electrons, protons, and neutrons are *bundled in a hierarchy of different-sized "containers"*.

For example, when you have "a package" of one proton, one neutron, and one electron in the atom, you can be certain that the element will be hydrogen. When you have two protons, two neutrons, and two electrons spinning in an atom, your atom will be helium. And when you have a package of ninety-five protons, the atom of the element will be americium.

Listed below is a small snapshot showing the various "proton-element" (container) configurations:

Periodic Classification of the Elements

Number of Protons (Atomic Number)	Element Name (Container)	Number of Protons (Atomic Number)	Element Name (Container)
1	Hydrogen	11	Sodium
2	Helium	12	Magnesium
3	Lithium	13	Aluminum
4	Beryllium	14	Silicon
5	Boron	15	Phosphorus
6	Carbon	27	Cobolt
7	Nitrogen	47	Silver
8	Oxygen	79	Gold
9	Fluorine	92	Uranium
10	Neon	95	Americium

Yes, Nature keeps track of the same essence (*the natural process of tallying*) by assigning unique container sizes to discrete units of measure!

Just as it is possible to decode the atomic structure of elements through atomic numbers, so with DNA we can decipher every single component of every gene—every letter, so to speak—in that yard-long *code* of life.

Of course, mapping out the *genome-sequencing* is not a simple matter of stretching our genes and reading off the base-pair combinations; but just as with the *numerical-sequence* and the *atomic-number sequence*, every single component of every gene, like every physical quantity, has a very specific description and location in the long chain of Being—in the long chain of Invariance.

We do similar counting with money. We can count in 100-dollar bills, 20-dollar bills, quarters, nickels, or pennies. For example, we might have five 20-dollar bills, or 400 quarters of the same 100-dollar currency.

Each law of physics expresses a quantity relationship; and because all of the laws are invariable and interrelated, each therefoi :, is an expression of one grand relationship among the physical laws. Hence, just as different building blocks of currency represent a *sequence* of different denominations, forms, and values (nickels, dimes, quarters, etc.), *so different building blocks of the very same essence* (Invariance) represent a hierarchical staircase (higher-level systems) of different physical quantities (natural units of reality, hierarchical ladder of quantization), such as time, space, matter, elements, planets, and galaxies.

There are over forty-five known physical quantities and over 2000 mathematical relationships that these quantities can enter into. Just as the Rosetta stone was used to decode the writing on a roll of ancient Egyptian papyrus, it is possible—with the tools of physics, disarmingly simple mathematical analysis, and high speed computers—not only to unify the fundamental physical quantities of time, space, force, electromagnetism, gravity, and so on, into one cohesive global network (like creating a planetary map of oceans, mountains, and cities), but also to break the awesome code of the hierarchical levels of the fundamental quantum-of-value of the same essence. (For a more detailed presentation, please refer to Appendix B.)

As the basic building blocks organize to form different parts, the physical quantities change. Just as bricks are joined to form walls, and walls give birth to a house; so the coin of the lowest value—the *smallest* physical quantity (the *smallest fundamental* building block of nature)—the moment of inertia—becomes space, space forms mass, mass makes time, time becomes energy, energy gives birth to gravity, and so forth.

Starting with the smallest fundamental building block of Invariance (the smallest fundamental quantum-of-value—natural unit of reality)— the moment of inertia—a partial list of the Periodic Classification of the Physical Quantities (as displayed in Figure 5 and Tables 2 and 3 in Appendix B) follows in order of size:

Periodic Classification of the Physical Quantities

Natural Units of Reality (physical quantities)		Dimensional Units
Moment of Inertia	10^{-57}	Kg-m^2
Volume (Space)	10^{-41}	m^3
Angular Momentum	10^{-36}	kg-m^2/sec
Mass	10^{-31}	kilograms
Time	10^{-22}	seconds
Electric Flux	10^{-19}	coulombs
Energy	10^{-14}	joules
INVARIANCE	0	dimensionless
Magnetic Potential	10^3	amperes
Velocity	10^8	meters/second
Electric Field	10^{19}	volts/meter
Pressure	10^{27}	new/m^2
Gravity	10^{30}	m/sec^2
Angular Acceleration	10^{43}	rad/sec^2

The hard tools of science and mathematics are showing us that *the very same essence is everywhere, but is packaged in different building blocks — in different-sized containers* of physical quantities, particles, elements, chemical and organic compounds, molecules, micro-organisms, plants, animals, and man.

ALL
PEOPLE
ARE YOUR
IMMEDIATE FAMILY

What all of these scientific breakthroughs add up to is a very important finding of fundamental significance. Although the giant trail blazers (Moses, Buddha, Trismagistus, Zoroaster, Krishna, Jesus, Heisenberg, Planck, Dirac, Schroedinger, Einstein, Eddington, and Bohm), crossed the high mountains of cosmic consciousness and, through personal observation and verification, informed us of the golden coast of *connectedness* of *unity* among us. Using mathematical forms of great simplicity and beauty, we can now prove with physics and mathematics, that indeed EVERYTHING IS INTIMATELY LINKED, THROUGH THE INVARIABILITY OF QUANTITIES, into One Essence.

Furthermore, we can prove that each of us exists in the same, single, all-embracing multidimensional system of hidden symmetries and fundamental physical quantities, the relationships and properties of which are determined by their function in the whole. That is, *beneath the plane of ordinary subjective perspective, the entire structure of existence is an Invariable Hierarchical Chain of Being.*

Putting it simply, the everyday world of trees, human beings, plants, animals, and galaxies is connected to everything else in such a way that careful study of any individual element could theoretically reveal detailed information about other elements in the universe. Metaphorically, the universe resembles a *dictionary*—wherein every word's definition also contains definitions of every other word in the dictionary.

Using the religious nomenclature: *God* [*I Am What I Am*] is everywhere, but in different manifestations.

Basically, at the heart of it all—we are (*through* time, space, gravity, and so on) invisibly connected (fused) into a single framework underlying the physical reality. It is God. *It is YOU!!!* The world is our lifeblood and all of its citizens are our immediate family. They are You. You are they. We are One Essence. We are the Creator who, in a sense, has taken a nap for a few billion years; who slept through the Big Bang scenario, the formation of the stars, through the development of the higher forms of consciousness, and finally to where we are in the last five thousand years; to this time where we are slowly waking up—unfolding to ever-increasing richness and glory.

Earlier we quoted Eddington's essential insight of modern physics:

> We have found that where science has progressed the farthest, the *mind has but regained from nature that which the mind has put into nature.* We have found a strange footprint on the shores of the unknown. We have devised profound theories, one after another, to account for its origin. At last, we have succeeded in reconstructing the creature that made the footprint. And *Lo! it is our own.*[164]

As we have seen from the various quotes of the East and the West, for thousands of years, mystics, saviors, and saints, through personal insight, have been restating the same wonderful song of oneness—of God within us of living unity among us.

This is one of the most precious moments in our conscious history. Like a twentieth-century Moses, the field of the physical sciences is utilizing the hard verification tools of physics and mathematics to finally help part the modern-day Red Sea of blood, nuclear bombs, widespread violence, pain, and bondage. This utilization will lead to more freedom, productivity, service-excellence—to One Family.

Such an experience of unity was shared by a physicist:

It was Holy Thursday and there before me on a table lay the unleavened bread. From within the bread I heard a voice: "This is my body." It was the Christ and he affirmed again as did Albert Einstein, David Bohm, and others more recently that we are all one body.

New vistas of increasing certainty, knowledge and tremendous opportunity are opening up before us as never before. We are learning that human beings are capable of much more than we thought. New knowledge—in the role of a beneficial leader—will be forging improved connections for enormous energy releases, higher levels of attainment, human closeness, prosperity, and peace. A very exciting phase in our adventure is emerging. We are all part of it.

Together, let us sum up some of the key messages:

1. Know the truth and the truth shall set you free.

2. The world is but forgetfulness of God.

3. Physics, through physical quantities and the laws of physics, measures the same fundamental essence: Invariance.

4. The very same essence is everywhere, but it is packaged in different natural units of measure—in different-sized containers of physical quantities.

5. The physical quantity-sequence and global relationship among the physical quantities are outlined (Appendix B).

6. You are a part of the physical quantities; you are a part of Invariance.

7. Everything is part of everything else—*the observer and the observed are fundamentally one.*

8. *You are the Creator* himself/herself. You have assumed human form, and are entertaining yourself in this limited spacetime movie on Earth. *You are me, I am you! You are looking at yourself through your brother's eyes!*

9. Great opportunities are opening up before us.

I AM
WHO
I AM

Joy! Joy! Joy!
I am the smile, the sky, and the sorrow.
I am the little ant and the graceful sparrow.
I am the blue-eyed child;
The fragrance you love;
The beat of your heart;
And the woman you hug.
I am the law, the beginning, and the end
Everyone and everything is me;
And there is no one else but me.
I am gazing out of every face, including yours.
Indeed, I Am Who I Am.

Remember,
Before this journey you knew everything.
There was no time or space, no birth or death.
There was nothing further to be experienced.
You spoke of yourself to yourself.
Timeless eternity and ceaseless bliss seemed boring.
You decided to create an illusion;

To limit the spectrum of your perception.
You have divided yourself into many forms.
Now you appear to yourself disjointed:
As a flower, as a waterfall, or as your own brother.
Yet, you made certain that the pressure of self-discovery
Takes you back to your original knowledge.
Do not be uneasy, my love,
About this great excursion.
Do not be troubled, my joy,
With so many different faces and forms.
They are all carved out of the same
One Light of Invariance.
They are you!

Rejoice, rejoice, rejoice!
You will be enraptured in your blissful glory.
Yes, my Light; yes, my Love; yes, my Joy.
You will perceive the Triumphant Absolute
In your own being.

Know yourself.
Press onward to deeper understanding
And knowledge of truth.
Achieve, through purity of heart,
Love of your neighbor, detachment from results,
And stillness of the mind, limitless freedom.
Cherish each opportunity
To serve and to love.
Each One teach One.
Through your contacts at work,
While traveling
Bring this message to others.
It is a luminous road of radiant beauty,
Happiness, splendor, and light.
It is a captivating pilgrimage
You have prepared for yourself.
It is Joy.

It is Love.
It is Light.
It is You!

Thank you. I love you!

Orest

APPENDIX A

Summary of Insights: Invariance (I)

Augustine, Saint
Lord, I have sought you in all the temples of the
world and lo, I found you within myself . . .
If a man does not find the Lord within himself,
he will surely not find Him in the world.[147]

Baba, Meher
Who am I? And to that Question
there is only one Answer—I am God![91]

You are infinite. You are really Everywhere;
but you think you are the body, and therefore
consider yourself limited.[91]

I am in your own souls!
Why see you not?
In every breath of yours am I.[92]

"Indeed I am this All, All This is Mine"—
This word resoundeth ever from within![94]
You are Your-Self the Thinker, and this world
But Your own Thought, and God but
Your-Self.[94]

The God-realized knows himself to be God as
surely as a man knows himself to be a man.[114]

Bernard, Saint

Who is God? I can think of no better
answer than, He who is.[88]

If you call God good, or great, or
blessed, or wise, or anything else of this
sort, it is inclined in these words, namely,
He is.[88]

Bible, The

You are gods, all of you sons of
the Most High. (Ps. 82:6)

You are the light of the world. (Matt. 5:14)

Is it not written in your law, "I have said,
'YOU ARE GODS'?" (John 10:34)

Whoever has seen me has seen the Father. (John 14:9)

I am in the Father and the Father is in me. (John 14:11)

I am in my Father, and you in me, AND I IN YOU. (John 14:20)

They are not of the world, anymore than I belong to the world.
(John 17:16)

Father, I pray . . . that they may be one, as you, Father, are in me, and
I in you; I pray that they may be in us . . . I living in them, you living
in me—that their unity may be complete. (John 17:20–21, 23)

In Him we live and move and have our being. (Acts 17:28)

Are you not aware that you are the temple of God, and that the Spirit of God dwells in you? (1 Cor. 3:16)

Your body is a temple of the Holy Spirit, who is within. (1 Cor. 6:19)

We many though we are, are one body. (1 Cor. 10:17)

The body is one and has many members, but all the members, many though they are, are one body. (1 Cor. 12:12)

If all the members were alike, where would the body be? (1 Cor. 12:19)

There are, indeed, many different members, but one body. (1 Cor. 12:20)

If one member suffers, all the members suffer with it; if one member is honored, all the members share its joy. (1 Cor. 12:26)

You, then, are the body of Christ. Every one of you is a member of it. (1 Cor. 12:27)

All of us . . . are being transformed from glory to glory into his very image by the Lord who is the Spirit. (2 Cor. 3:18)

The life I live now is not my own; Christ is living in me. (Gal. 2:20)

Each one of you is a son of God. (Gal. 3:26)

All are one in Christ Jesus. (Gal. 3:28)

One body and one Spirit. (Eph. 4:4)

God is love, and he who abides in love abides in God, and God in him. (1 John 4:16)

Blake, William
I am in you and you in me.[20]

Bohm, David
What we perceive through the senses as empty space is actually the plenum, which is the ground for the existence of everything, including ourselves.[29]

The things that appear to our senses are derivative forms and their true meaning can be seen only when we consider the plenum, in which they are generated and sustained.[29]

The entire universe (with all its "particles," including those constituting human beings, their laboratories, observing instruments, etc.) has to be understood as a single undivided whole.[85]

Carey, Ken

The Creator and Creation are joined in physical flesh; for it is One Life that pulsates within everybody.[65]

I beat with every throb of your heart,
Feel with every touch of your hand,
Cry your every tear,
Breathe your every breath.
I am never far away.[87]

For I am the first and last,
the beginning and the end, the Creator of
all that is and of all that is to be.[137]

My potential is infinite, my Being eternal.
All creation is an ever-unfolding picture
of what I conceive. The star fields are my canvas,
humans are my brushes, biology is my paint.[137]

Catherine of Genoa, Saint

Then of herself she neither works nor speaks
nor wills nor feels nor hears nor understands,
neither has she of herself the feeling of
outward or inward, where she may move.[72]

The state of this soul is then a feeling of such
utter peace and tranquillity that it seems to
her that her heart, and her bodily being, and
all both within and without is immersed in an ocean
of utmost peace; from whence she shall never come forth for
anything that can befall her in this life.[72]

And she stays immovable, imperturbable, impassible.
ZG0-000
So much so, that it seems to her in her human and spiritual
nature, both within and without, she can feel no other
thing than sweetest peace. And she is so full of peace
that though she press her flesh, her nerves, her bones,
no other thing comes from them than peace.[72]

My Me is God, nor do I recognize any other Me except my God
himself.[142]

Cidade Caleixnese

The kingdom of heaven is within you, and whosoever shall know
himself shall find it.[111]

D'Espagnot

The notion of reality existing independently of man has no meaning whatsoever.[16]

Dirac, Paul

All matter is created out of some imperceptible substratum.[27]

It [imperceptible substratum] uniformly fills all space and is undetectable by any observation.[27]

It [imperceptible substratum] appears as NOTHINGNESS—immaterial, undetectable, and omnipresent.[27]

It [imperceptible substratum] is a peculiarly material form of nothingness out of which all matter is created.[27]

Eckhart, Meister

I am that which I was and shall remain, now and forevermore.[33]

In thus breaking through, I perceive what God and I are in common.[33]

I am the immovable which moves all things.[33]

The seed of God is in you.[115]

132

Gandhi, Mahatma

He is a personal God to those who need His touch.[89]

He is the purest essence.[89]

To me God is Truth and Love, God is Ethics and Morality.[89]

God is the source of light and life and yet He is above and beyond all these.[89]

He is the greatest democrat the world knows, for he leaves us unfettered to make our own choice between evil and good.[89]

Gospel of Thomas, The

The kingdom is within you and it is without you.[74]

Halliday, David

The building blocks of physics are the physical quantities in terms of which the laws of physics are expressed.[159]

All physical laws are the same in all reference frames. Observers in different frames [of reference] may obtain different numerical values for measured physical quantities, but the relationship between the measured quantities, that is, the laws of physics, will be the same for all observers.[160]

James, William

In mystic states we both become one with the Absolute and we become aware of our oneness.[40]

John of the Cross, Saint

The heavens are mine,
The earth is mine, and the nations are mine!
Mine are the just, and the sinners are mine;
Mine are the angels and the Mother of God;
All things are mine,
God himself is mine and for me,
Because Christ is mine and all for me.[149]

What do you ask for,
What do you seek for, O my soul?
All is yours—all is for you.[149]

Krishna, Gopi
This unimaginable Cosmic Intelligence
is present at every spot in the Universe,
and our whole personality, ego, mind,
intellect and all—is but an infinitely small
bubble blown on this boundless ocean.[67]

Maharshi, Ramana
Reality is only one and that is the Self,
The seer, the objects, and the sight,
all are the Self only.[43]

Mechthild of Magdeburg:
I am in you and you are in me.
We cannot be closer.
We are two united,
poured into a single form by an
eternal fusion.[145]

Moslem Sufis
The "world" is but forgetfulness of God.[90]

There's naught within your robe but
God Himself, the knower and the known
are but the same. He who knows God is God;
God knows Him-Self.[146]

I saw You not before—I see You now,
Belov'd! You peep forth from every face!
I saw You not before—behind the clouds
Beloved! You did not hide. I see you now![152]

Muhammad
I, verily the I All-One, am One, am God,
There is no other God than I (the Self,
The Universal all-pervading Self).[109]

Planck, Max
In the last analysis, we ourselves are part of nature.[17]

Resnick, Robert
The building blocks of physics are the
physical quantities in terms of which the
laws of physics are expressed.[159]

All physical laws are the same in all reference frames.
Observers in different frames [of reference]
may obtain different physical quantities, but
the relationship between the measured quantities,
that is, the laws of physics, will be the same
for all observers.[160]

Al-Rumi, Jalaluddin
The Beloved is all that lives.[105]

I am you and you are me.[143]

Schroedinger, Erwin
I am God Almighty.[13]

ATMAN = BRAHMAN (the personal self equals the omnipresent,
all-comprehending, eternal self).[13]

Our perceiving self is nowhere to be found within the world-picture: because it itself is the world-picture.[42]

Subramuniya
At first you feel light shining within you.[119]

Tasawwuf
The wise see in their heart the face of God,
And not in images of stone and clod!
Who in themselves, alas! can see Him not,
They seek to find Him in some other spot.[96]

Teresa of Avila, Saint
God implants Himself in the interior of that soul
in such a way that, when it returns to itself,
it cannot possibly doubt that God has been in it
and it has been in God.[71]

Tzu, Chuang
I and all things in the Universe are one.[37]

Upanishad, The Svetastara
Thou art woman. Thou art man.
Thou art the youth and the maiden too.
Thou art the dark-blue bird
and the green parrot with red eyes.
Thou art the seasons and the seas.
Having no beginning.[86]

Upanishads, The
In the beginning this world was merely non-being.[25]

It was existent.[26]

This whole world is Brahma.[78]

Atman alone is the whole world.[79]

You are he.[80]

I myself am he![81]

The world is his; indeed, he is the world itself.[82]

This Soul is the overlord of all things, the king of all things.[83]

I am the Infinite;
What you are, that same am I;
You are all This;
I am all This.[144]

Vedas, The
Truly, You are Godhead Yourself.[100]

The countless heads, eyes, ears, and hands and feet of living beings
are all parts of One Man.[106]

The progeny of Adam, all are parts
And limbs of one and the same organism,
Risen from the Same Essence, everyone;
And can it be, while one limb is in pain,
That other limbs should feel at restful ease?[107]

Vyasa
Everything rests upon me.
I am the taste of water,
The light of the sun and the moon.[77]
I am the sound in ether and the ability in man.
I am the original fragrance of the earth.
I am the heat in fire.
I am the life of all that lives.
I am, in one sense, Everything.[77]

Wheeler, John
The universe does not exist "out there" independent of us.[15]

Wilber, Ken
All things, including subatomic particles, are ultimately made of God.[84]

Wingate
I AM the Cosmos, the Universe. Everything That Is . . .
I AM the First Cause.

I AM the Last Effect.
I AM Every Cause and Every Effect.
I AM Spirit.
I AM Soul.
I AM Matter.
I AM Everyone and Everything.
I AM THE ONE.
I AM ALSO THE MANY.
AND WHATEVER IT IS THAT SAYS I AM,
I AM THAT I AM.[66]

Summary of Insights: From God to Man (II)

Athanasius, Saint
The Divine Word became man.[22]

Bohm, David
The entire universe of matter as we generally observe it is to be treated as a comparatively small pattern of excitation.[29]

This excitation pattern is relatively autonomous and gives rise to approximately recurrent stable and separable projections into a three-dimensional explicate order of manifestation.[29]

Dewey, John
Intelligence has descended from its lonely isolation at the remote edge of things, whence it operated as Unmoved Mover, and ultimate good, to take its seat in the moving affairs of men.[34]

Dirac, Paul
... the creation of matter leaves behind it a "hole" in this substratum which appears as antimatter.[27]

Eckhart, Meister
When I came out of the Godhead into multiplicity . . . [33]

Irenaeus, Saint
God the Logos became what we are . . . [21]

Muktananda, Swami
God Himself assumes human forms and lives in the world.[30]

Muller, Robert
We are cosmic matter come alive, partaking of the divine character of our Creator.[19]

The soul of the universe, incarnated in a human being, lost much of its qualities and became imperfect.[32]

Rama, Swami
The Brahman [Creator] became many.[24]

Upanishads, The
In the beginning this world was merely *non-being* It developed. It turned into an egg.[26]

Summary of Insights: Relativity (III)

Baba, Meher
People do not know who they really are.[91]

You are blind.
Without true eye,
And see Me not.[92]

He who is absent, far away from God—
His heart can only say: "God is" somewhere.[93]

Who may I take for guide upon the Way
One who himself away from it does stray?
He is content to say, "God is," while I
Am desolate till I "God am" can say![93]

Just think! If the Creator you do find,
Can His creation still remain behind?[94]

The soul that is not God-realized
experiences itself as finite and is constantly
troubled by the opposites of joy and sorrow.
But the soul that has realization is lifted
out of them and experiences the Infinite.[120]

Bible, The

They know not, neither do they understand;
they go about in darkness;
all the foundations of the earth are shaken. (Ps. 82:5)

Yet like men you shall die;
and fall like any prince. (Ps. 82:7)

Reform your lives! (Matt. 4:17)

Whatever came to be in him, found life, life for the light of men.
THE LIGHT SHINES on in darkness, a darkness that did not
overcome it. (John 1:4–5)

Davis, Paul

The most important scientific discovery of our age is that the physical universe did not always exist.[154]

Eckhart, Meister

A man has many skins in himself,
covering the depths of his heart.
Man knows so many things;
He does not know himself.[103]

Why, thirty or forty skins or hides,
Just like an ox's or bear's,
So thick and hard, cover the soul.
Go into your own ground
And learn to know yourself there.[103]

Goodness needeth not enter into the soul,
for it is there already, only it is unperceived.[104]

Einstein, Albert

He experiences himself, his thoughts and feelings, as something
separated from the rest—a kind of optical delusion of his consciousness. This delusion is a kind of prison for us . . . [14]

Gospel of Thomas, The

If you do not know yourselves,
then you are in poverty
and you are the poverty.[74]

Huxley, Aldous

[It is] because we are unaware that the Kingdom of Heaven is within
us, that we behave in the generally silly, the often insane, the sometimes criminal ways.[99]

The world is an illusion.[117]

Our business is to wake up. We have to find ways in which to detect
the whole of reality in the one illusory part which our self-centered
consciousness permits us to see.[117]

We must not live thoughtlessly, taking our illusion for the complete
reality, but at the same time we must not live too thoughtfully in the
sense of trying to escape from the dream state.[117]

Jeans, Sir James

Things are not what they seem; it is the general recognition that we
are not yet in contact with ultimate reality. We are still imprisoned
in our cave, with our backs to the light, and can only watch the
shadows on the wall.[101]

Maharshi, Ramana

Why should you bear your load on the head when you are traveling in a train? . . . You are not lessening the burden of the train by
keeping it on your head but only straining yourself unnecessarily.[43]

Milarepa
Remove the rust of wrong ideas.[136]

Moslem Sufis
No bar guards His palace-gateway,
No veil screens His Face of Light—
You are my heart! By your own self-ness
Are enwrapped in darkest night.[90]

Neng, Hui
When non-enlightened Buddhas are no other than ordinary beings;
when there is enlightenment, ordinary beings at once turn into
Buddhas.[97]

Rama, Swami
Manyness or plurality is but a transformation assumed by the
Absolute.[24]

Teresa of Avila, Saint
Oh human blindness!
How long, how long shall it be before the dust is removed from
our eyes?[35]

Upanishads, The
In the beginning this world was merely non-being.[25]

It was existent. It developed. It turned into an egg. It was split asunder.
One of the two egg-shell parts became silver, one gold.[26]

Wingate
I am the one.
I am also the many.
And whatever it is that says I am,
I am that I am.[66]

Summary of Insights: From Man to God (IV)

Ashtavakra

Be constantly engaged in work for the welfare of others.[59]

Athanasius, Saint

The divine word became man that we might become gods.[22]

Baba, Meher

If you look within and experience your own soul in its true nature, you will realize that you are infinite and beyond all creation.[91]

He who has found the Loved One in Him-Self For him God is not he, nor You, but I.[93]

If you find God, then you have found all things![94]

The soul discovers that it has always been the Infinite Reality, and that its looking upon itself as finite during the period of evolution and spiritual advancement was an illusion.[120]

The soul also finds that the infinite knowledge and bliss that it enjoys have been latent in the Infinite Reality from the beginning of time and that they became manifest at the moment of realization.[120]

Baba, Sai

It is through discrimination and renunciation that man understands who he really is, namely God himself.[118]

Basil the Great

Through His aid, hearts are lifted up, the weak are led by the hand, and they who are advancing are brought to perfection. By His illumination of those who are purified from all defilement, He makes them spiritual by fellowship with Him.[140]

Hence comes to them unending joy, abiding in God, being made like unto God, and which is the highest of all, being made God.[140]

Bible, The

The moment you eat of it you will be like gods who know what is good and what is bad. (Gen. 3:4)

The Lord God said: "See! The man has become like one of us, knowing what is good and what is bad!" (Gen. 3:22)

Rise, O God; judge the earth, for yours are all the nations. (Ps. 82:8)

You must be made perfect as your heavenly Father is perfect. (Matt. 5:48)

As often as you did it for one of my least brothers, you did it for me. (Matt. 25:40)

If you live according to my teaching, you are truly my disciples; then you will know the truth, and the truth will set you free. (John 8:31–32)

The man who has faith in me will do the works I do, and greater far than these. (John 14:12)

[Father, I pray] . . . that all may be one as you, Father, are in me, and I in you; I pray that they may be [one] in us, . . . I living in them, you living in me—that their unity may be complete. (John 17:20–21, 23)

Indeed, the whole created world eagerly awaits the revelation of the sons of God . . . because the world itself will be freed from its slavery . . . and share in the glorious freedom of the children of God. (Rom. 8:19,21)

Glorify God in your body. (1 Cor. 6:20)

You are my children, and you put me back in labor pains until Christ [God] is formed [realized, matured] in you. (Gal. 4:19)

There was a time when you were darkness, but now you are light in the Lord. (Eph. 5:8)

Awake, O sleeper, arise from the dead, and Christ will give you light. (Eph. 5:14)

Blake, William

If the doors of perception were cleansed, everything would be seen as it is, infinite.[41]

Bohm, David

The things that appear to our senses are derivative forms and their true meaning can be seen only when we consider the plenum, in which they are generated and sustained, and into which they must ultimately vanish.[29]

Carey, Ken

It is One Life that pulsates within everybody. We have now only to be joined in consciousness, in awareness, and all will be fulfilled according to the prophecy.[65]

Carpenter, Edward

If you inhibit thought (and persevere), you come at a region of consciousness below or behind thought . . . and a realization of an altogether vaster self than that to which we are accustomed.[39]

So great, so splendid is this experience, that it may be said that all minor questions and doubts fall away in the face of it.[39]

Catherine of Genoa, Saint

When the loving kindness of God calls a soul from the world, He finds it full of vices and sins; and first He gives it an instinct for virtue, and then urges it to perfection, and then by infused grace leads it to true self-naughting, and at last to true transformation.[72]

Catherine of Siena, Saint

If you will arrive at a perfect knowledge and enjoyment of Me, the Eternal Truth, you should never go outside the knowledge of yourself.[70]

By humbling yourself in the valley of humility you will know Me and yourself.[70]

Cidade Caleixnese
And you shall know that you are in the City of God, and you are the City.[111]

de Chardin, Teilhard
Someday, after mastering the winds and the waves, the tides and gravity, we shall harness the energy of love. And then, for the second time in the history of the world, man will have discovered fire.

The men of the future will form, in some way, but one single consciousness.[126]

The single act of assimilation and synthesis that has been going on since the beginning of time will then at last be made plain, and the universal Christ will blaze out like a flash of lightning in the storm clouds of a world whose slow consecration is complete.[126]

Eckhart, Meister
In breaking through I am more than all creatures.[33]

Eddington, Arthur
The mind has but regained from nature that which the mind has put into nature.[23]

We have succeeded in reconstructing the creature that made the footprint. And Lo! it is our own.[23]

Einstein, Albert
If one were to take that goal out of its religious form and look merely at its human side, one might state it perhaps thus: Free and responsible development of the individual, so that he may place his powers freely and gladly in the service of mankind.[4]

Our task must be to free ourselves from this prison by widening our circle of compassion to embrace all living creatures and the whole of nature in its beauty.[14]

Gospel of Thomas, The
Love your brother as your own soul, guard him as the pupil of your eye.[61]

When you know yourselves, then you will be known. And you will be aware that you are the sons of the Living Father.[74]

Let him who seeks not cease from seeking until he finds.[75]

Huxley, Aldous

That is why we can attain to the unitive knowledge of God only when we become in some measure Godlike, only when we permit God's kingdom to come by making our own kingdom go.[116]

We are saved, we are liberated and enlightened, by perceiving the hitherto unperceived good that is already within us, by returning to our eternal ground and remaining where, without knowing it, we have always been.[102]

We must continually be on our watch for ways in which we may enlarge our consciousness. We must not attempt to live outside the world, which is given us, but we must somehow learn how to transform it and transfigure it.[117]

One must find a way of being in the world while not being of it. A way of living in time without being completely swallowed in time.[117]

It is only by becoming Godlike that we can know God—And to become Godlike is to identify ourselves with the divine element which in fact constitutes our essential nature.[138]

Irenaeus, Saint

God the Logos became what we are, in order that we may become what he himself is.[21]

James, William

This overcoming of all the usual barriers between the individual and the Absolute is the great mystic achievement.[40]

John of the Cross, Saint

Go forth and exult in your glory,
Hide yourself in it, and rejoice,
And you shall obtain all desires of your heart.[149]

Krishna, Gopi

Probably no other spectacle, not even the most incredible supernormal performance of mystics and mediums, so clearly demonstrates the existence of an All-Pervading, Omniscient intelligence behind the infinitely varied phenomena of life as the operations of a freshly awakened Kundalini.[67]

Maharaj, Tukaram

I went to look for God, but didn't find God.
I myself became God. In this very body, God
revealed Himself to me.

Maharshi, Ramana

Reality is only one and that is the Self.[43]

The seer, the objects, and the sight, all are the Self only.[43]

If, on the other hand, you surrender yourself and recognize your individual self as only a tool of the Higher Power, that Power will take over your affairs along with the fruits of actions.[43]

Merton, Thomas

To live with the true consciousness of life centered in another is to lose one's self-important seriousness and thus to live life as "play" in union with a Cosmic Player.[45]

Find joy and spontaneity in everything.[45]

To live life selflessly is to live in joy, realizing by experience that life itself is love and a gift.[45]

Be a channel through which the Supreme Giver manifests His love in the world.[45]

Milarepa, Jetsun

It is through resting one's mind . . . that Buddhahood is realized.[36]

Muktananda, Swami

The veil which made you see duality drops away, and you experience the world as a blissful play of Kundalini, a sport of God's energy.[124]

A being who has attained this state does not have to close his eyes and retire to a solitary place to get into samadhi.[124]

Whether he is meditating, eating, bathing, sleeping, whether he is alone or with others, he experiences the peace and joy of the Self. Whatever he sees is God, whatever he hears is God, whatever he tastes is God's.[124]

We do not meditate to attain God, because we have already attained Him. We meditate so that we can become aware of God manifest within us.[124]

Meditate on your Self, honor your Self, worship your Self, for God dwells within you as you.[124]

Muller, Robert

The effort of human beings should be to strive . . . to the perfection of the soul and to feel part of the mysterious flow and throbbing of the universe.[32]

Neng, Hui

When there is enlightenment, ordinary beings at once turn into Buddhas.[97]

Paul, Pope

Stand in admiration, rejoice; we have become Christ.[150]

Rumi, Jalaluddin

I died as a mineral and became a plant.
I died as a plant and rose as an animal.
I died as an animal and I was a man.
Yet once more I shall die as man,
to soar with the blessed angels;

But even from angelhood I must pass on.
When I have sacrificed my angel soul,
I shall become what passes the conception
of man! Let me then become Non-Existent,
For Non-Existence sings,
"To Him shall we return."[121]

Santayana, George
Live as much as may be in the eternal.[56]

Let him clean better, if he can, the windows of his soul, that the variety and beauty of the prospect may spread more brightly before him.[41]

Schroedinger, Erwin
Our perceiving self is nowhere to be found within the world-picture: because it itself is the world-picture.[42]

When a man knows his true Self for the first time, something else arises from the depths of his being and takes possession of him. That something is behind the mind; it is infinite, divine, eternal.[44]

The greatest power is at the command of the man who has penetrated to his Inmost depth.[44]

What is the use of knowing about everything else when you do not know yet who you are?[44]

I have become God.[98]

Shankara
Deliverance is not achieved by repeating the word *Brahman,* but by directly experiencing Brahman.[60]

Subramuniya
As you release desires and cravings through daily meditation, the external mind releases its hold on your awareness and you dive deeper, fearlessly, into the center of this blazing avalanche of light beyond form and formlessness.[119]

As you come out of that Samadhi, you realize you are the spirit, the life force of all.[119]

Teresa, Mother
In serving the poorest we directly serve God.[113]

Tzu, Chuang
A man does not see himself in running water but in still water.[37]

Vedanta
Why will you wander in the wilderness!
You who are seeking God!
Yourselves are He!
You need not search!
He is you, verily![95]

The mystical classics have, as has been said,
neither birthday nor native land; perpetually
telling of the unity of man with God, their speech
antedates language, and they do not grow old.[40]

Wheeler, John A.
The universe not only must give rise
to life, but . . . once life is created,
it will endure forever, become infinitely
knowledgeable, and ultimately mold the universe
to its will . . . thus man—or Life—will be not
only the measure of all things, but their creator
as well.[127]

Wingate
We begin to realize that we are joined in the most deeply intimate communion with every other Soul in the Cosmos. That we are joined with the One Soul. That It is in us. That we and the One Soul are One.[64]

APPENDIX B

The Nature of Reality

Whether it is the cuneiform numerals of the ancient Babylonians, the hieroglyphics of the Egyptian papyri, or the measurements made by different observers, each is a brilliant achievement and admirable deed, on the reality tally of spacetime.

The Big Bang came and passed away. So did the Sumerians, Moses, Newton, Lincoln, and Einstein. You were born. On the surface, the *passing* of spacetime appears as if indeed everything is fluid—everything is relative. Our intention is not to challenge relativity, but to consider another dimension of how nature keeps an accounting on her notched sticks of time.

First and foremost, *ALL Nature appears to be invariable.* As noted earlier, all physical laws are identical in all reference frames. Observers in different frames may obtain different numerical values for measured physical quantities, but the relationship between the measured quantities, that is, the laws of physics, will always be the same for all observers.

One can equate our reality to a *calculator,* in which the inner structure of the calculator is *hard-wired,* that is, *invariable,* unchanging. However, one "calculation" is relative compared to another.

Furthermore, the *order* of numbers (the physical quantities, table of elements, etc.) in the calculator's "display" window are arranged in a *fixed sequence.* If we start with "identical" conditions in a calculator and add a set of identical numbers to it, we will always have the same end result. The *hard-wired* design of the "reality calculator" allows us to verify the various physical laws and derive physics and mathematics.

Earlier, we mentioned that before the Big Bang and our excursion into multiplicity, all scenarios, like a prerecorded phonograph record, were known to us. We made a change. Now we listen to short "music segments" on our individual record. While the self-discovery goes on and the "historic" lullaby progresses, we would like to shed some light on how the reality hard-wire connections between the physical systems (quantities or *natural units of measurement*) are arranged and what the grand relationship between those systems is (for illustrative purposes, please refer to Figure 3). Here, we have a very simple seesaw, the kind on which two children sit at opposite ends of a plank supported in the middle and swing up and down.

The *central support* (the dimensionless zero state of the physical law, the Paul Dirac nothingness, "where space and time and every known dynamic principle collapses") is in the middle of the plank, which throughout the book we have referred to as the *Invariance Plenum,* or the zero stillness plenum, which supports the physical reality. It is the *central reference,* from which the reality counting (please see Figure 4) and *the physical quantity measurements by dimensions (numerical units of measure) start* (please see Figure 5; for definitions of quantities, please see Table 7). The central support also serves as a *transformation interface for natural units of measure* (physical quantities—please see Figure 6) and *reality-shift center* between numerical values for measured quantities (please see Figure 7). Mathematically, *the central support of the plank can be represented as an Equal Sign* ("=") in physical equations or as a *Zero* ("0") in numerical values.

The *letters* on both sides of the plank (please see Figure 5) represent the building blocks of nature—the natural units of measure (physical quantities, properties of higher level systems).

The "−" and "+" on both ends of the plank is the *direction of measurement* from the central support.

Nature

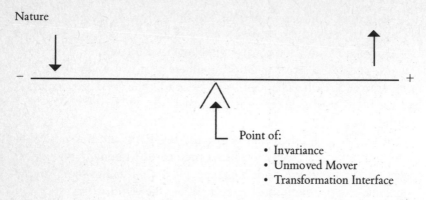

Point of:
- Invariance
- Unmoved Mover
- Transformation Interface

Figure 3

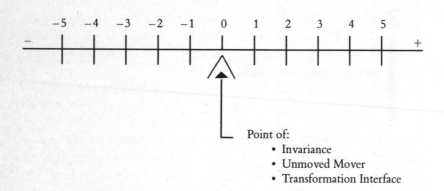

Point of:
- Invariance
- Unmoved Mover
- Transformation Interface

Figure 4

The relationship among the physical quantities on the plank (please see Figure 6) is that of the *universal ratios* of nature—that which can be measured with the laws of physics.

The *sequence* and *separations* between the letters on the plank, *like numbers on an engineering slide rule* (please see Figure 5), represent *the actual arrangement and distances on the quantity slide rule of nature—the grand relationship among the physical quantities*. Notice that the plank, whether in the condition of Figures 3–6, when it is immovable (the zero state *prior to* the movement and manifestation), or in the up-and-

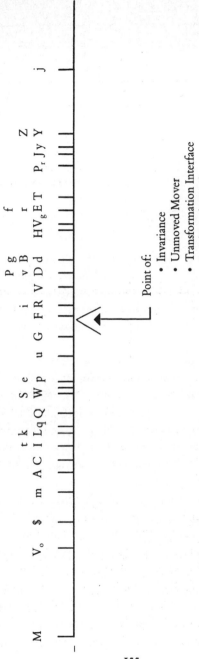

Invariance Ladder

(Periodic Classification of the Physical Quantities)

Point of:
- Invariance
- Unmoved Mover
- Transformation Interface
- "=" (Equals Sign)

Figure 5

155

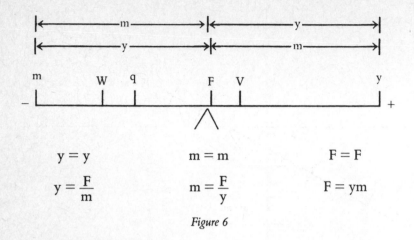

$y = y$ $m = m$ $F = F$

$y = \dfrac{F}{m}$ $m = \dfrac{F}{y}$ $F = ym$

Figure 6

down swing, when children play in Figure 7, is identical. That is, *the separation between the physical quantities and the relationships between those quantities* (on the plank and nature) will be identical no matter how fast the children move up and down on the plank. Simply put, *the plank does not change* — the quantity slide rule of the laws of physics is the same in all reference frames. The children playing in Figure 7 illustrates that what changes, as we rotate the frames of reference, are the quantity *transformations* and the numbered value for measured physical quantities.

Note another important fact: *as we rotate the frame of reference from Figure 5 to Figure 8, the reality changes. Physical quantities that were one thing in Figure 5 become something else in Figure 8.* For example, mass (m), when taken through spacetime rotation, in Figure 8, becomes energy (W); or magnetic flux density (B), when moved through spacetime rotation, becomes electric potential (V); and so forth.

As with every single component of DNA, or the table of elements, where there are *very specific arrangements* and configurations among the myriad genome-sequencings and the atomic and subatomic particles, so with the physical quantities, there are very exact relationships and arrangements. Table 1 depicts the numerical sequence and global relationship among numbers. Table 2 shows the physical *quantity sequence* and the *global relationship* among the *physical quantities.* There is nothing novel about Table 1, but it can serve as a stepping stone for understanding Tables 2–5.

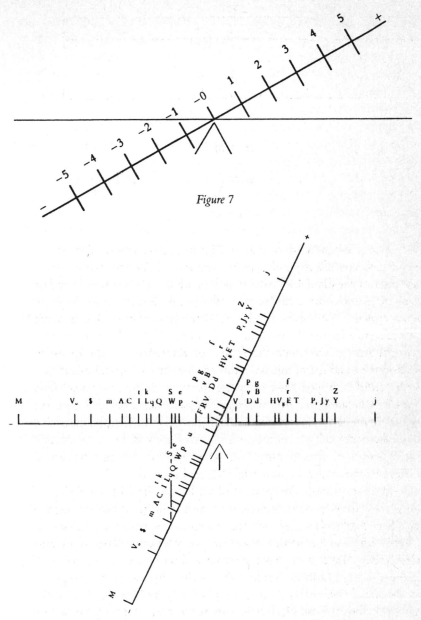

Figure 7

Figure 8

Please note just as two in Table 1 can equal $2 = 8/4 = 10/5 = 14/7 \ldots$ so the physical quantity of electric potential (V) in Table 2 can equal $V = q/C = Ri = W/q$. As with numbers (in Table 1 and Figure 4), there can be more than one way to express the same answer, so with physical quantities (in Table 2 and Figure 5), there are many physical relationships that will yield identical quantity.

Furthermore, because with numbers (please see Table 1 and Figure 4) we understand the numerical *value,* we can arrange them in numerical sequence. With physical quantities the challenge is a bit more involved. That is, time, space, gravity, and so forth, unlike stones that can be assembled in different piles and compared for size (or the atomic elements, which can be weighted and measured), the physical quantities interpenetrate each other; i.e., time, space, gravity can have the same space, the same time, the same gravity. Had it not been for the various laws of physics that have already been tested and verified, the next step for a *global mapping of the physical quantities* would not have been possible. Tables 2–5, like numbers on an engineering slide rule (please see Figure 5), show the actual *sequence* and the grand relationship (separation, distances) among the physical quantities at the Invariance level.

Earlier (please see page 111) we have indicated that every part of reality and every physical relationship (proportion, connection ratio, organization) among the physical quantities is invariable; i.e., is valid in all reference frames. This means Invariance provides the common link, the cohesive structure, and the universal coupling of all laws of physics. That is, there is an *invariable order, scale, arrangement, and succession* among ALL the physical quantities. *If that invariable link did not exist, we would not be able to verify the laws of physics.*

The next question: How can we determine what the global organization and universal relationship among the physical quantities is? Let us try an exercise here.

Please place *each* individual equation from Table 2 on a 3 × 5 card. For example, when U (moment of inertia) equals $= mS = F/j = W/y$, please create three separate cards with: $U = mS$; $U = F/j$; $U = W/y$.

As mentioned, there are over forty-five known physical quantities. When we cross multiply the physical quantities (45 × 45) we will have over 2000 individual quantity relationships on 3 × 5 cards. Now please attach these equation cards with masking tape to a wall. Next, you will need a computer and a program that can help you speed up your computing process. Specifically, because the physical equations on the 3×5 cards are in *equational equilibrium, all 2025 physical equations cross-check simultaneously.*

That is, given the cohesive structure of the invariable relationship of the physical quantities, one must determine the *physical value* for each quantity that satisfies *all* laws of physics *simultaneously;* i.e., *THE NUMERICAL VALUES OF THE ENTIRE TABLE 2 SYSTEM OF EQUATIONS MUST NUMERICALLY CROSS–CHECK.* We must find a set of forty-five numbers that, when substituted into each of the forty-five quantities (in our 3×5 cards), will cross-check among all Table 2 relationships. This test is tremendously important, for *just as all physical laws interconnect among themselves, so the numbers, when substituted into the equations, must connect among themselves.*

To determine the numerical value for each quantity that satisfies all the laws of physics simultaneously, an interactive method may be employed. That is, successive approximations for the numerical values may be tested on the entire Table 2 system of equations. With each repetition, closer approximations of the solution are attained. This process is repeated *until the numerical value for each quantity, one that satisfies the entire system of equations, is achieved.*

Now I am assuming you have gone past the first try, that is, you have found (like Archimedes of Syracuse with King Hieron's crown) a set of forty-five numbers that will satisfy all of the Table 2 quantity relationships.

Next, because each quantity is invariant and not equal to any other quantity, one must establish the Physical Quantity Sequence, i.e., the sequence of physical quantities based upon their physical quantum of measure. Please sort each card by number (i.e., 1, 2, 3 and so on, with the smaller numbers on top and the larger ones on the bottom). Notice the sequential arrangement of quantities. You might want to pencil on the back of each card its relative position to other cards.

Then, repeat the exercise again. Pick another number. Go through the code-breaking substitution with numbers, like you would with crossword puzzles and letters. When you have found a new combination of numbers that satisfy *all* the equations, go through the card-sorting process again. Note the sequential arrangement of quantities. Pencil the relative card position of each quantity.

After you have tried this exercise a number of times, you will notice an interesting phenomenon. You will find that after each sorting of your 3 × 5 cards, *the quantities always fall in the same Table 2 sequence.* Just as with atoms, in the table of elements, we can determine the size of each atom, or with DNA's the code of life by deciphering every single component of every gene map, so *with the laws of physics we can determine the size and the relative sequence of each quantity.*

Question: How can we mix the units of measure (dimensions) among quantities? Remember the example on page 115 from our arithmetic classes: We can bundle apples with apples in boxes, truckloads, and shiploads; physical quantities are interchangeable; they are the same essences but packaged in different container sizes. That is, just as with apples, we can count in *units* of boxes, truckloads, or shiploads, so with physical quantities *we count* in different units of measurement! Hence, *when we were sorting the "container" [physical quantity] sizes in our experiment, we were sorting* (boxes, truckloads, and shiploads) *collections of the same essence by higher level systems of quantities.*

Once the physical quantities sequence has been established, one can very easily do transformations (as, for instance, with an engineering slide rule) among physical quantities. For example, "y" distance from the invariable (transformation) *zero center* on the right side of Figure 6 is the same as the distance from F to m, i.e., $y = y$ or $y = F/m$. This is also true when $m = m$ or "m" from the center in Figure 6 is the same distance as the distance between "F" and "y" (F/y). This principle is very useful, for *now we can create a Quantity Slide Rule for physics.*

There is one more point to consider. Earlier we stated that on the surface it appears as if everything is indeed fluid—or relative.

When we consider the hard interconnectedness that exists with physical quantities in Table 2 and a similar scenario that is present with *dimensions* of those quantities, as we study Tables 3–5, it becomes evident that mathematical logic, the entire universe of time, space, and matter, all historical events, everything we generally see and experience daily, like a prerecorded movie, is *permanently stored,* similar to the invariable laws of physics, in every bit of reality, in every bit of invariance.

To be able to rediscover and *read* the engraving of this "movie," our minds somehow generate small patterns of excitation that give rise to what we see and experience.

The things that appear to our senses," as we noted earlier, "are derivative forms and their true meaning can be seen only when we consider the plenum..." And "the entire universe of matter as we generally observe it is to be treated as a comparatively small pattern of excitation..." that "gives rise to approximately recurrent stable and separable projections into a three-dimensional explicate order of manifestation."[165] What is suggested here is that *physical quantities, the laws of physics, and all dimensional relationships and historical events are invariable.*

When you look at a prerecorded phonograph record, is it relative? No. The record is invariable. However, the song on one groove compared to a song on another groove could be relative. The same principle applies to nature. Like a prerecorded phonograph record, from the beginning to the end, all songs (events, experiences) are there. We are only entertaining ourselves with particular "segments" of music.

Table 6 extends the information of Tables 3–5. It shows that just as quantities (Table 2) portray immovable oneness among the various *natural units of reality, so dimensions portray immovable oneness* among the various units of measure. Table 6 was generated by substituting different numbers into the *entire* system of equations in Table 2 and then sorting them by size. Starting with the smallest measure and moving to the largest, we have a symmetrical union throughout the quantity spectrum. *If this symmetrical arrangement among the units of measure did not exist, we would not be able to come up with the laws of physics nor verify invariability.*

Hence, observers in different frames may obtain different numerical values for physical quantities, but the relationships among the measured quantities, that is, the laws of physics and *the relationships among dimensions and units of measure will always be the same for all observers.*

In the special theory of relativity published by Albert Einstein in 1905, the mass (m) of a particle *increases* with its velocity (v) according to the relation:

$$m = \frac{m_o}{\sqrt{1 - (v/c)^2}} \quad \text{or} \quad \frac{m_o}{\sqrt{c^2 - v^2}} = \frac{m}{c}$$

where (m_o) is the mass of the particle when at rest with respect to the observer, and (c) is the speed of light.

When one takes into account not just the quantities of velocity and mass, but the 45 quantities with the 45 ways that these quantities interact with each other in 2025 physical equations *simultaneously,* one discovers that mass always *decreases* as velocity *increases* (please see Table 6). There is a disparity.

When we are in New York City we are in a stable state, a fixed relationship between city buildings and streets (as located on a map). When we are in Tokyo we have another stable state, a fixed relationship between Tokyo's buildings and streets. Table 3 demonstrates how the physical quantities relate to each other on one physical plane, e.g., how the streets and buildings are positioned to each other in New York City; whereas Table 4 demonstrates how the physical quantities relate to each other on another physical plane, e.g., how the streets and buildings are arranged in Tokyo.

Because the reality is *invariable* we can take one physical relationship (i.e. velocity × time = distance) and transform one stable state (travel from New York) to another stable state (Tokyo). In everyday calculations, that is exactly what we are doing—we are shifting our point of reference.

However, when shifting the reference point we can not transform the same quantity two different ways in the *same* equation and hope to wind up in the same place, e.g., we can not travel at ten miles per hour while we are going at the speed of light and expect to be at the identical location. That is exactly what Einstein has done in his equation with transforming velocity (v) and the speed of light (c) at the same time. That is why there is a discrepancy between the special theory of relativity and the unified quantities theory.

Nor can we increase the mass (m_o) and velocity (v_o) of the particle when at rest to some new velocity (v) and mass (m) level with this type of relationship:

$$\text{old mass} \rightarrow \frac{m_o}{v_o} = \frac{m}{v} \leftarrow \text{new mass} \\ \text{old velocity} \rightarrow \quad\quad \leftarrow \text{new velocity}$$

moreover, we can not do this:

$$\frac{m_o}{\sqrt{c^2 - v^2}} = \frac{m}{c} \leftarrow \text{the problem}$$

Please note, no matter what happens to the new mass (m), Einstein's new velocity (c) is always constant—an impossible condition when considering all laws of physics (Table 2) in totality.

For a quick verification of the above statements we suggest an experiment by keeping track of the magnetic flux density (B), the electric flux (q), the velocity (v) of a particle and its radius (S) and then computing the particle mass according to this relationship: $qvB = mv^2/S$ or $m = SqB/v$.

Below we suggest these particle dimensions from Tables 2–6:

B (tesla)	q (coul)	v (m/sec)	S (meters)		m (kg)
4.81×10^{10}	1.60×10^{-19}	2.99×10^8	3.54×10^{-14}	=	9.10×10^{-31}
3.32×10^9	1.76×10^{-17}	3.59×10^7	1.02×10^{-12}	=	1.67×10^{-27}
1.9×10^6	8.2×10^{-12}	1.0×10^5	1.22×10^{-8}	=	1.9×10^{-18}

You may want to perform these verifications with other quantity settings, using Tables 2 to 6.

In studying Figure 5, one notices that when a physical quantity on the right of the point of Invariance increases, all other quantities on the right of the point of Invariance also will *increase* in size, while all quantities on the left of the point of Invariance will *decrease,* i.e., when velocity (v) increases (goes up from Figure 5 to Figure 8) volume (V_o), mass (m), time (t) and charge (q) will decrease (go down from Figure 5 to Figure 8); and conversely, when mass (m), volume (V_o) and time (t) increase, velocity (v), electromagnetism (H and E) and acceleration (y) will decrease in size.

Further, with our present understanding, velocities greater than the speed of light can not exist. When one studies the gravitational potential (V_g) in *which* light travels (like a person walking in a moving train) one notices that the gravitational potential equals velocity squared ($V_g = v^2$) (please see Tables 2 and 3). Now we have to find new ways of measuring the moving train.

TABLES

Table 1

NUMERICAL QUANTITIES TABLE

Sequence and transformations of numbers by numerical value from the smallest to the largest.

2 = two = $8/4$ = $10/5$ = $14/7$
3 = three = $12/4$ – $6/2$ = $21/7$
4 = four = $16/4$ = $20/5$ = $8/2$ = 2×2
5 = five = $10/2$ = $15/3$ = $20/4$
6 = six = $12/2$ = 3×2 = $18/3$
7 = seven = $21/3$ = $14/2$
8 = eight = 2×4 = $16/2$
9 = nine = 3×3 = $18/2$
10 = ten = 2×5 = $2 \times 15/3$
12 = twelve = 4×3 = 6×2
14 = fourteen = 2×7 = $4 \times 7/2$
15 = fifteen = 3×5 = $6 \times 5/2$
16 = sixteen = 2×8 = 4×4
20 = twenty = 4×5 = 2×10
21 = twenty-one = 3×7

Table 2
PHYSICAL QUANTITIES TABLE

Sequence and transformations of quantities by physical quantum-of-measure from the smallest to the largest.

Note: *Sources for equations with '=' sign are listed in footnote 166. '= :' indicates new equations. These equations may exist in print, the author is unaware of their publication.*

M = Moment of inertia = mS^2 = FS/j = FS^2/y = W/j

U = Inertia (linear) = $: mS$ = $: F/j$ = $: W/y$

V_o = Volume = m/d = W/P_r

$\$$ = Angular momentum = IS = MT

h = Planck constant = $I\lambda$ = W/f = Wk

P_m = Elect. dipole moment = qS

m = Mass = dV_o = F/y = I/v = qE/y = $F\Delta t/\Delta v$ = qBt = M/S^2

A = Area = i/J = Q/B = F/P_r = q/D = Q/Hu

C = Capacitance = q/V = $: eS$

t = Time = v/y = m/qB = FS/P = $1/T$

I = Momentum (linear) = mv = $\$/S$ = W/v = h/λ

k = Period = λ/v = $1/f$ = h/W

L = Self inductance = $v\Delta t/\Delta i$ = $: uS$

q = Electric flux = F/E = W/V = CV = ym/E = F/vB

Q = Magnetic flux = AHu = BA

S = Displacement = V/E = i/H = V/Bv = gA/G = Mj/F = $(My/F)^{1/2}$ = $\$/I$ = y/j

W = Work (energy) = qV = V_oP_r = Iv = iBA = qES = h/k = hf = Mj

λ = Wavelength = v/f = vk = h/I

e = Permitivity = D/E = $1/uv^2$ = $1/K$ = C/S

p = Electric resistivity = E/J = $1/g$ = V/H = $: RS$

u = Permeability = B/H = $1/ev^2$ = B^2/P_r = B/Dv = Q/HA = L/S

G = Conductance = i/V = P/V^2 = $1/R$ = gA/S = i^2/P

F = Force = qE = AP_r = P/v = my = $\Delta W/\Delta S$ = qBv = $m\Delta v/\Delta t$ = BSi = $I/\Delta t$

R = Resistance = V/i = $1/G$ = P/i^2 = V^2/P

i = Magnetic potential = V/R = P/V = JA = $\Delta q/\Delta t$ = F/BS = $(P/R)^{1/2}$ = HS

V = Electric potential = ES = q/C = Ri = W/q = i/G = P/i = $(P/G)^{1/2}$ = $(PR)^{1/2}$ = $L\Delta i/\Delta t$ = BSv = YA

D = Electric flux density = Ee = H/v = q/A = P_r/E = Bve

v = Velocity = E/B = $f\lambda$ = $1/(ue)^{1/2}$ = P/F = H/D = $\Delta S/\Delta t$ = I/m = $(p_r/d)^{1/2}$ = W/I = F/qB = V/BS = $: TS$

P = Power = Vi = i^2R = Fv = Iy = V^2/R = V^2G = i^2/G = $\Delta W/\Delta t$

d = Density = m/V_o = P_rue = HB/v^2 = j/Z

B = Magnetic flux density = E/v – Q/A = P_r/H = Hu = F/Si

g = Electric conductivity = J/E = H/V = iS/AV

K = Coulomb's constant = $: 1/e$ = $: S/C$

Table 2 (Continued)
PHYSICAL QUANTITIES TABLE

$\mathbf{H}$ = Magnetic field intensity = $\mathbf{Dv}$ = $\mathbf{B}/u$ = $i/\mathbf{S}$ = Q/Au = $P_r/\mathbf{B}$

$\mathbf{V}_g$ = Gravitational potential = W/m = $\mathbf{v}^2$

$\mathbf{E}$ = Electric field intensity = $\mathbf{Bv}$ = F/q = J/g = $\mathbf{D}/e$ = $p\mathbf{J}$ = $\Delta V/\Delta \mathbf{S}$ = my/q = $P_r/\mathbf{D}$

$\mathbf{r}$ = Reluctance = $\mathbf{S}/uA$ = i/Q

f = Frequency = $\mathbf{v}/\lambda$ = $1/k$ = W/h

$\mathbf{T}$ = Angular velocity = P/W = $\mathbf{F}/\mathbf{I}$ = : $\mathbf{v}/\mathbf{S}$ = $1/t$ = $\mathbf{v}/\mathbf{y}$ = $\sqrt{\mathbf{j}}$ = qB/m

P_r = Pressure = F/A = $e\mathbf{E}^2$ = $\mathbf{HB}$ = $\mathbf{ED}$ = W/V_o = $u\mathbf{H}^2$ = $\mathbf{B}^2/u$

$\mathbf{J}$ = Current density = i/A = $\mathbf{Eg}$ = $\mathbf{E}/p$ = $\mathbf{H}/\mathbf{S}$

$\mathbf{y}$ = Acceleration (linear) = $\mathbf{F}/m$ = $q\mathbf{E}/m$ = $\mathbf{F}\mathbf{S}^2/\mathbf{M}$ = $\Delta \mathbf{v}/\Delta t$ = $\mathbf{v}\mathbf{T}$

$\mathbf{Y}$ = Voltage density = : V/A = $\mathbf{E}/\mathbf{S}$

$\mathbf{Z}$ = Constant of universal gravitation = : $\mathbf{T}^2/d$ = : $\mathbf{y}^2/P_r$

$\mathbf{j}$ = Angular acceleration = $\mathbf{y}/\mathbf{S}$ = $\mathbf{F}/\mathbf{S}m$ = Zd = $\mathbf{T}^2$ = $W/\mathbf{M}$

Note: *1) moment of inertia (rotational inertia) divided by displacement equals linear inertia* ($\mathbf{M}/\mathbf{S}$ = $\mathbf{U}$)*; and 2) linear inertia divided by displacement equals mass (*$\mathbf{U}/\mathbf{S}$ = m*).*

Table 3

PHYSICAL CONSTANTS WITH
ELECTRON MASS AS FRAME OF REFERENCE

Sequence of physical constants by value from the smallest to the largest. See footnotes 166 and 167. Also, see Table 7 for the definitions of symbols.

	Sym	*Computed*		*(SI units)*
Moment of inertia	**M**	1.142296387	$\times 10^{-57}$	kg-m^2
Inertia (linear)	**U**	3.22580052	$\times 10^{-44}$	kg-m
Volume	V$_o$	4.440418326	$\times 10^{-41}$	m^3
Angular momentum	**$**	9.670706669	$\times 10^{-36}$	kg-m^2/sec
Planck constant	h	6.62617656	$\times 10^{-34}$	joule sec
Elect. dipole moment	p$_m$	5.673553053	$\times 10^{-33}$	col m
Mass (electron)　(&) m		9.10953507	$\times 10^{-31}$	kilograms
Area	A	1.253956848	$\times 10^{-27}$	m^2
Capacitance	C	3.135378865	$\times 10^{-25}$	farads
Time	t	1.181192261	$\times 10^{-22}$	sec
Momentum	**I**	2.73096991	$\times 10^{-22}$	kg-m/sec
Period	k	8.093295287	$\times 10^{-21}$	sec
Self inductance	L	4.449909298	$\times 10^{-20}$	henrys
Electric flux　(&) q		1.602189292	$\times 10^{-19}$	coul
Magnetic flux	Q	6.035932503	$\times 10^{-17}$	webers
Displacement	**S**	3.54112531	$\times 10^{-14}$	m
Work (energy)	W	8.18724182	$\times 10^{-14}$	joules
Wavelength　(&) λ		2.426308886	$\times 10^{-12}$	m
Permitivity　(&) e		8.85418782	$\times 10^{-12}$	far/m
Electric resistivity	p	1.334049206	$\times 10^{-11}$	ohm-m
Permeability　(&) u		1.256637012	$\times 10^{-6}$	henry/meter
Conductance	G	2.654418733	$\times 10^{-3}$	mhos
INVARIANCE	=	**0**		**dimensionless**
Force	**F**	2.31204515		newtons
Resistance	R	3.76730313	$\times 10^{2}$	ohms
Magnetic potential	i	1.356417015	$\times 10^{3}$	amperes
Electric potential	V	5.110034101	$\times 10^{5}$	volts
Electric flux density	**D**	1.27770688	$\times 10^{8}$	coul/sqm
Velocity　(&) **v**		2.99792458	$\times 10^{8}$	m/sec
Power	P	6.931337202	$\times 10^{8}$	watts
Density	d	2.051503807	$\times 10^{10}$	kg/m cu
Magnetic flux density	**B**	4.8135098944	$\times 10^{10}$	tesla
Electric conductivity	g	7.495975378	$\times 10^{10}$	mhos/m

Table 3 (Continued)
PHYSICAL CONSTANTS WITH
ELECTRON MASS AS FRAME OF REFERENCE

Coulomb's constant	K	1.129409064	$\times\ 10^{11}$	joule m/coul^2
Magnetic field intensity	**H**	3.830468862	$\times\ 10^{16}$	amp/m
Gravitational potential	V$_g$	8.987551787	$\times\ 10^{16}$	joules/kg
Electric field intensity	**E**	1.443053678	$\times\ 10^{19}$	volts/meter
Reluctance	r	2.247236815	$\times\ 10^{19}$	amp-t/web
Frequency (linear)	f	1.235590652	$\times\ 10^{20}$	hertz
Angular velocity	**T**	8.466022281	$\times\ 10^{21}$	rad/sec
Pressure	P$_r$	1.843799612	$\times\ 10^{27}$	new/sq-m
Current density	**J**	1.081709484	$\times\ 10^{30}$	amp/sq-m
Acceleration (lineal)	**y**	2.5380495627	$\times\ 10^{30}$	m/sec^2
Voltage density	**Y**	4.075127553	$\times\ 10^{32}$	volt/sq-m
Const. univ. grav.	Z	3.493707056	$\times\ 10^{33}$	nt-m^2/kg^2
Angular acceleration	**j**	7.167353145	$\times\ 10^{43}$	rad/sec^2

Table 4
PHYSICAL CONSTANTS WITH
PROTON MASS AS FRAME OF REFERENCE

	Sym	Computed	(SI units)	
Moment of inertia	**M**	1.756	$\times 10^{-51}$	kg-m^2
Volume	V$_o$	1.076	$\times 10^{-36}$	m^3
Angular momentum	**$**	6.163	$\times 10^{-32}$	kg-m^2/sec
Mass	(&) m	1.673	$\times 10^{-27}$	kilograms
Area	A	1.050	$\times 10^{-24}$	m^2
Capacitance	C	1.441	$\times 10^{-22}$	farads
Time	t	2.849	$\times 10^{-20}$	sec
Momentum	**I**	6.015	$\times 10^{-20}$	kg-m/sec
Period	k	1.233	$\times 10^{-18}$	sec
Self inductance	L	5.635	$\times 10^{-18}$	henrys
Electric flux	q	1.765	$\times 10^{-17}$	coul
Magnetic flux	Q	3.491	$\times 10^{-15}$	webers
Displacement	**S**	1.025	$\times 10^{-12}$	m
Work (energy)	W	2.163	$\times 10^{-12}$	joules
Wavelength	λ	4.435	$\times 10^{-11}$	m
Permitivity	e	1.406	$\times 10^{-10}$	far/m
Electric resistivity	p	2.026	$\times 10^{-10}$	ohm-m
Permeability	u	5.4996	$\times 10^{-6}$	henry/meter
Conductance	G	5.05657	$\times 10^{-3}$	mhos
INVARIANCE	=	**0**		**dimensionless**
Force	**F**	2.1108046		newtons
Resistance	R	1.9776260	$\times 10^2$	ohms
Magnetic potential	i	6.1952369	$\times 10^2$	amperes
Electric potential	V	1.22518	$\times 10^5$	volts
Electric flux density	**D**	1.6813781	$\times 10^7$	coul/sqm
Velocity	**v**	3.59593587	$\times 10^7$	m/sec
Power	P	7.5903179	$\times 10^7$	watts
Density	d	1.55476	$\times 10^9$	kg/m cu
Magnetic flux density	**B**	3.32514	$\times 10^9$	tesla
Electric conductivity	g	4.93486	$\times 10^9$	mhos/m
Magnetic field intensity	**H**	6.0461	$\times 10^{14}$	amp/m
Gravitational potential	V$_g$	1.293	$\times 10^{15}$	joules/kg
Electric field intensity	**E**	1.1957	$\times 10^{17}$	volts/meter
Reluctance	r	1.7745	$\times 10^{17}$	amp-t/web
Frequency (linear)	f	8.1075	$\times 10^{17}$	hertz
Angular speed	**T**	3.5094	$\times 10^{19}$	rad/sec

Table 4 (Continued)
PHYSICAL CONSTANTS WITH
PROTON MASS AS FRAME OF REFERENCE

	Sym	*Computed*	*(SI units)*	
Pressure	P_r	2.0104	$\times 10^{24}$	new/sq-m
Current density	J	5.9006	$\times 10^{26}$	amp/sq-m
Acceleration (linear)	y	1.2620	$\times 10^{27}$	m/sec^2
Voltage density	Y	1.1669	$\times 10^{29}$	volt/sq-m
Const. univ. grav.	Z	7.9214	$\times 10^{29}$	nt-m^2/kg^2
Angular acceleration	j	1.2312	$\times 10^{39}$	rad/sec^2

Table 5

PHYSICAL CONSTANTS WITH
D QUARK CHARGE AS FRAME OF REFERENCE

	Sym	Computed	(SI units)	
Moment of inertia	**M**	4.097	$\times 10^{-59}$	kg-m^2
Volume	V$_o$	4.200	$\times 10^{-42}$	m^3
Angular momentum	**$**	1.250	$\times 10^{-36}$	kg-m^2/sec
Mass	m	1.574	$\times 10^{-31}$	kilograms
Area	A	2.603	$\times 10^{-28}$	m^2
Capacitance	C	7.488	$\times 10^{-26}$	farads
Time	t	3.279	$\times 10^{-23}$	sec
Momentum	**I**	7.745	$\times 10^{-23}$	kg-m/sec
Period	k	2.5014	$\times 10^{-21}$	sec
Self inductance	L	1.436	$\times 10^{-20}$	henrys
Electric flux (&)	q	5.342	$\times 10^{-20}$	coul
Magnetic flux	Q	2.339	$\times 10^{-17}$	webers
Displacement	**S**	1.613	$\times 10^{-14}$	m
Work (energy)	W	3.811	$\times 10^{-14}$	joules
Wavelength	λ	1.231	$\times 10^{-12}$	m
Permitivity	e	4.641	$\times 10^{-12}$	far/m
Electric resistivity	p	7.066	$\times 10^{-12}$	ohm-m
Permeability	u	8.9011	$\times 10^{-7}$	henry/meter
Conductance	G	2.28344	$\times 10^{-3}$	mhos
INVARIANCE	=	**0**		**dimensionless**
Force	**F**	2.3617540		newtons
Resistance	R	4.3793638	$\times 10^2$	ohms
Magnetic potential	i	1.6288999	$\times 10^3$	amperes
Electric potential	V	7.1335455	$\times 10^5$	volts
Electric flux density	**D**	2.05198903	$\times 10^8$	coul/sqm
Velocity	**v**	4.9200	$\times 10^8$	m/sec
Power	P	1.16198	$\times 10^9$	watts
Density	d	3.7480	$\times 10^{10}$	kg/m cu
Magnetic flux density	**B**	8.9864	$\times 10^{10}$	tesla
Electric conductivity	g	1.4153	$\times 10^{11}$	mhos/m
Magnetic field intensity	**H**	1.0096	$\times 10^{17}$	amp/m
Gravitational potential	V$_g$	1.764	$\times 10^{17}$	joules/kg

Table 5 (Continued)
PHYSICAL CONSTANTS WITH
D QUARK CHARGE AS FRAME OF REFERENCE

	Sym	*Computed*	*(SI units)*	
Electric field intensity	E	4.4213	$\times\ 10^{19}$	volts/meter
Reluctance	r	6.9631	$\times\ 10^{19}$	amp-t/web
Frequency (linear)	f	3.9977	$\times\ 10^{20}$	hertz
Angular speed	T	3.0494	$\times\ 10^{22}$	rad/sec
Pressure	P_r	9.0725	$\times\ 10^{27}$	new/sq-m
Current density	J	6.2573	$\times\ 10^{30}$	amp/sq-m
Acceleration	y	1.5003	$\times\ 10^{31}$	m/sec^2
Voltage density	Y	2.7403	$\times\ 10^{33}$	volt/sq-m
Const. univ. grav.	Z	2.4810	$\times\ 10^{34}$	nt-m^2/kg^2
Angular acceleration	j	9.3013	$\times\ 10^{44}$	rad/sec^2

Table 6
PHYSICAL RELATIONSHIPS IN NATURE

Quantities:

mass (kg)	time (sec)	charge (coulombs)	energy (joules)	Invariance (dimensionless)	force (newtons)	D (coul/sq m)	velocity (m/sec)	B (web/sq m)	density (kg/m³)
7.5×10^{70}	5.4×10^{51}	2.2×10^{44}	7.7×10^{30}	0	1.4×10^{-1}	7.5×10^{-20}	1×10^{-20}	6.3×10^{-26}	8.6×10^{-97}
1.4×10^{53}	6.3×10^{38}	1.8×10^{33}	1.4×10^{23}	0	2.2×10^{-1}	4.5×10^{-15}	1×10^{-15}	1.3×10^{-19}	8.9×10^{-73}
2.7×10^{35}	7.4×10^{25}	1.5×10^{22}	2.7×10^{15}	0	3.7×10^{-1}	2.7×10^{-10}	1×10^{-10}	2.5×10^{-13}	9.3×10^{-49}
5.2×10^{17}	8.6×10^{12}	1.2×10^{11}	5.2×10^{7}	0	6.1×10^{-1}	1.7×10^{-5}	1×10^{-5}	5.0×10^{-7}	9.6×10^{-25}
3.5×10^{3}	3.9×10^{2}	1.6×10^{2}	3.5×10^{1}	0	9.1×10^{-1}	1.1×10^{-1}	1×10^{-1}	5.5×10^{-2}	1.6×10^{-5}
0	0	0	0	0	0	0	0	0	0
2.8×10^{-4}	2.6×10^{-3}	6.1×10^{-3}	2.9×10^{-2}	0	1.1	9.0×10^{0}	1×10^{1}	1.8×10^{1}	6.3×10^{4}
1.9×10^{-18}	1.2×10^{-13}	8.2×10^{-12}	1.9×10^{-8}	0	1.6	6.0×10^{4}	1×5^{5}	1.9×10^{6}	1.0×10^{24}
1.7×10^{-27}	2.8×10^{-20}	1.8×10^{-17}	2.2×10^{-12}	0	2.1	1.7×10^{7}	proton	3.3×10^{9}	1.9×10^{36}
4.5×10^{-29}	2.0×10^{-21}	1.8×10^{-18}	4.5×10^{-13}	0	2.2	4.5×10^{7}	1×10^{8}	1.2×10^{10}	2.6×10^{38}
9.1×10^{-31}	1.2×10^{-22}	1.6×10^{-19}	8.2×10^{-14}	0	2.3	1.3×10^{8}	electron	4.8×10^{10}	5.2×10^{40}
3.5×10^{-36}	1.4×10^{-26}	6.7×10^{-23}	3.6×10^{-16}	0	2.7	3.7×10^{8}	1×10^{10}	4.0×10^{12}	1.1×10^{48}
7.0×10^{-54}	1.6×10^{-39}	5.5×10^{-34}	7.0×10^{-24}	0	4.4	2.2×10^{14}	1×10^{15}	8.0×10^{18}	1.1×10^{72}
1.3×10^{-71}	1.8×10^{-52}	4.5×10^{-45}	1.3×10^{-31}	0	7.2	1.3×10^{19}	1×10^{20}	1.6×10^{25}	1.2×10^{96}

Dimensions:

Table 7
DEFINITION OF QUANTITIES

A	Cross-sectional area of conduction in meter square
B	Magnetic flux density (magnetic induction) in tesla
C	Capacitance in farads
λ	Wavelength in meters
D	Electric flux density in coulombs per square meter
d	Density in kilogram/meter-cube
E	Electric field intensity in volts per meter
e	Permitivity of free space in farads per meter
F	Force in newtons
f	Frequency (linear) of the motion in hertz
G	Conductance in mhos
g	Electric conductivity in mhos per meter
H	Magnetic field intensity in amp-meter
h	Planck constant in joule sec
i	Magnetic potential (Electric current) in amperes
I	Momentum (volume of magnetization) in kilogram-meters/second
J	Current density in amperes per square meter
j	Angular acceleration in radians/sec^2
L	Coefficient of self-inductance in henrys
K	Coulomb's constant of proportionality in joule met/coul^2
k	Period of a harmonic motion in seconds
M	Moment of (rotational) inertia in kg-m^2
m	Mass in kilograms
P	Electric power in watts
P_r	Pressure in newtons per square meter
p	Resistivity in ohm-meter
Pm	Electric dipole moment in coul-meter
Q	Magnetic flux in webers
q	Electric charge in coulombs
R	Resistance in ohms
r	Reluctance in ampere-turn per weber
S	Displacement (orbit radius) in meters
T	Angular velocity in radians/sec
t	Time in seconds
u	Permeability in henrys/meter

Table 7 (Continued)

U	Inertia (linear) in kilogram-meter
V	Electric potential (emf) in volts
V_g	Gravitational potential in joules/kg
V_o	Volume in meter cube
v	Velocity (linear) of motion in meters per second
W	Energy (work) in joules
Y	Voltage density in volt/sq-m
y	Acceleration in meters/sec.sq
Z	Constant of universal gravitation in $nt\text{-}m^2/kg^2$
$	Angular momentum in $kg\text{-}m^2/sec$
=	Invariance: the dimensionless zero state of the physical law—the central reference from which quantity measurements by dimensions start in units of quantities.

NOTES

All Bible quotes marked "GN" are from *Good News for Modern Man* (New York: American Bible Society, 1970); all other Bible quotes are from *The New American Bible* (Washington, D.C.: Confraternity of Christian Doctrine, 1970).

1. Giscard d'Estaing, in *U.S. News and World Report,* March 3, 1975, p. 34.

2. Kenneth Clark, *Civilization: A Personal View* (New York: Harper & Row, 1969), p. 344.

3. David Bohm, *Wholeness and the Implicate Order* (London: Ark Paperbacks Ltd., 1983), pp. 138–9.

4. Albert Einstein, *Ideas and Opinions* (New York: Crown Publishers, 1954).

5. Rene Descartes, "Rules for the Direction of the Mind," trans. Elizabeth S. Haldane and G R T. Ross, *The Great Books of the Western World* (Chicago: Encyclopedia Britannica, Inc., 1971), vol. 31, p. 17.

6. *The New Encyclopedia Britannica* (Chicago: Helen Hemingway Benton, 1973–4), vol. 2, p. 1016.

7. Fritz Buri, *Der Pantokrator, Ontologie und Eschatologie als Grundlage der Lehre von Gott* (Hamburg-Bergstedt: Herbert Reich, 1969), pp. 56–64.
   Geoffrey Hodson, *The Hidden Wisdom in the Holy Bible* (an examination of the idea that the contents of the Bible are partly allegorical), 3 vols. (Wheaton, Ill.: The Theosophical Publishing House); idem, *The Christ Life from Nativity to Ascension* (London: The Theosophical Publishing House, 1975); idem,

"Lecture Notes," *The School of Wisdom,* vol. II (Adyar, Madras: The Theosophical Publishing House, 1955).

Gerald Tranter, *The Mystery Teachings and Christianity* (Wheaton, Ill.: The Theosophical Publishing House, 1969).

R. C. Zaehner, *Matter and Spirit: Their Convergence in Eastern Religions, Marx and Teilhard de Chardin* (New York: Harper & Row, 1963), pp. 44–67.

8. *The Zohar* III, 1528, (Soncino ed., vol. V, p. 211). A good edition of the book of *The Zohar* is that by Christian Knorr von Rosenroth, with Jewish commentaries (Schulzbach, 1684). Reprints with additional index (Amsterdam 1714, 1728, 1722, 1805, 3 vols.). Later editions of *The Zohar* were published at Breslau (1866, 3 vols); Livorno (1877–8 in 7 parts), and Wilna (1882, 3 vols; 1882–3 in 10 parts).

9. Quoted in Geoffrey Hodson, *Hidden Wisdom,* p. 42.

10. Ibid., p. 97.

11. Origen, *Origenes Werke* (Leipzig, 1899–1925), 8 vols.

12. Origen, "Selectra Psalmos, Patrologia Graeca XII," *Origenes Werke.*

13. Erwin Schroedinger, *What Is Life?* (Cambridge: The MacMillan Company, 1946), p. 88.

14. Albert Einstein, in *The New York Post,* November 28, 1972.

15. Quoted in Henryk Skolimowski, "Global Philosophy as the Canvas for Human Unity," *The American Theosophist.* May 1983, p. 163.

16. Ibid., p. 163.

17. Max Planck, *Where Is Science Going?* (New York: Norton, 1932).

18. Rabbi Ben Zion Bokser, ed. and trans., *The Essential Writings of Abraham Isaac Kook* (Warwick, N.Y.: Amity House, 1988), pp. 167, 170.

19. Robert Muller, *A Planet of Hope* (Warwick, N.Y.: Amity House, 1985), p. 21.

20. Geoffrey Keynes, ed., *The Writings of William Blake* (London, 1925), 3 vols.

21. Saint Irenaeus, *Adversus Haereses,* Book V, ch. 28, 4, in *The Ante-Nicene Fathers,* vol. 1, A. Roberts and J. Donaldson, eds. (Grand Rapids: Eerdmans, 1958), p. 557.

22. Saint Athanasius, *De Incarnatione Verbi,* p. 25, 192B.

23. Werner Heisenberg, *The Physicist's Conception of Nature* (New York: Harcourt and Brace, 1955).

24. Swami Rama, *The Book of Wisdom* (Kanpur, India: Himalayan International Institute of Yoga, Science and Philosophy, 1972), pp. 4–5.

25. *The Thirteen Principal Upanishads* (London: Oxford University Press, 1971), p. 11.

26. Ibid., p. 11.

27. Richard F. Plzak, Jr., *Paradox East and West,* unpublished senior dissertation, M.I.T., 1973, p. 54.

28. Chu Ta-kao, trans., *Tao-te Ching* (Boston: Mandala Books, 1982), ch. 25.

29. Bohm, *Wholeness,* pp. 191–2.

30. Swami Muktananda, *Play of Consciousness* (New York: Harper & Row).

31. Athanasius, *De Incarnatione Verbi,* p. 25.

32. Muller, *A Planet of Hope,* p. 62.

33. Meister Eckhart, *Works,* trans. C. B. Evans (London, 1924).

34. John Dewey, *The Influence of Darwin on Philosophy* (New York, 1910), p. 55.

35. Saint Teresa of Avila, *The Interior Castle,* trans. and ed. E. Allison Peers (Garden City, N.Y.: Image Books, 1944), p. 154.

36. Jetsun Milarepa, *One Hundred Thousand Songs of Milarepa,* trans. and annotated Garma C. C. Chang (Boulder: Shambala, 1977), vol. 2, p. 437.

37. Chuang Tzu, *Musings of a Chinese Mystic* (London, 1920).

38. Edward Carpenter, *The Drama of Love and Death* (London: George Allen & Unwin Ltd.).

39. Og Mandino, *The Greatest Salesman in the World* (New York: Frederick Fell Publishers, 1973), pp. 58–62.

40. William James, *The Varieties of Religious Experience* (London: Longmans Green, 1919).

41. Quoted in Aldous Huxley, *The Perennial Philosophy* (New York: Meridian Books, 1968), p. 189.

42. Schroedinger, *What Is Life?* p. 218.

43. Arthur Osbourne, *Ramana Maharshi and the Path of Self-Knowledge* (New York: Samuel Weiser, 1973).

44. Ibid., pp. 20–21.

45. Thomas Merton, *The Asian Journal of Thomas Merton,* ed. Naomi Burton, Brother Patrick Hart, and James Laughlin (New York: New Directions Press, 1973).

46. Elizabeth Haich, *Sexual Energy and Yoga* (London: George Allen & Unwin Ltd.).
    Marilyn Ferguson, *The Brain Revolution* (New York: Taplinger Publishing Company, 1973).
    Gopi Krishna, *Kundalini: The Evolutionary Energy in Man* (Berkeley, Ca., 1970); idem, *The Awakening of Kundalini* (New York: Dutton, 1975); idem, *The Biological Basis of Religion and Genius* (New York: Harper & Row, 1972); idem, *Higher Consciousness: The Evolutionary Thrust of Kundalini* (New York: The Julian Press, Inc., 1974).
    Milarepa, *One Hundred Thousand Songs.*
    Swami Muktananda, *Kundalini: The Secret of Life* (South Fallsburg, N.Y.: SYDA Foundation, 1987).

Vasant Rele, *The Mysterious Kundalini* (India: D. B. Taraporevala Sons & Co.).

Lee Sannela, M.D., *Kundalini—Psychosis or Transcendence?* (San Francisco: Sannela, 1976).

Swami Maharaj Vishnu Tirtha, *Devatma Shakti,* India.

John White, ed., *The Highest State of Consciousness* (New York: Doubleday, 1972); idem, *Kundalini, Evolution, and Enlightenment* (New York: Anchor Books/Doubleday, 1978).

47. Keith Dowman, trans., *Sky Dancer: The Secret Life and Songs of the Lady Yeshe Tsogyel* (London: Routledge and Kegan Paul, 1984).

48. Ibid., p. 156.

49. Ibid., p. 119.

50. Ibid., pp. 7–8.

51. *The Gospel of Thomas,* Log. 22 (York, England: The Ebor Press, 1987), p. 24.

52. *The Zohar.* See Note 8 above.

53. Muller, *A Planet of Hope,* p. 29.

54. Donald J. Hawkins, ed., *Famous Statements, Speeches, and Stories of Abraham Lincoln* (Scarsdale, N.Y.: Heathcote Publications, 1981), p. 2.

55. Ibid., pp. 16, 38.

56. George Santayana, *Reason in Common Sense* (New York: Charles Scribner and Sons, 1927), p. 28.

57. Milarepa, *One Hundred Thousand Songs.*

58. Einstein, *Ideas and Opinions.*

59. Paul Brunton, *The Hidden Teaching Beyond Yoga* (New York: Samuel Weiser, 1972), p. 36.

60. Shankara, *Viveka-Chudamani ("The Crest Jewel of Wisdom").*

61. *The Gospel of Thomas,* p. 26.

62. Haich, *Sexual Energy.*
Ferguson, *The Brain Revolution.*
Krishna, *Kundalini;* idem, *The Awakening;* idem, *The Biological Basis;* idem, *Higher Consciousness.*
Rele, *The Mysterious Kundalini.*
Sannela, *Kundalini.*
Vishnu Tirtha, *Devatma Shakti.*
White, ed., *The Highest State of Consciousness;* idem, *Kundalini.*

63. Edouard Schure, *The Great Initiates,* trans. from the French by Gloria Rasberry (San Francisco: Harper & Row, 1980), pp. 192–3.

64. Wingate, *Tilling the Soul* (New York: Aurora Press, 1984), pp. 65–7.

65. Ken Carey, *Vision* (Kansas City, Mo.: Uni Sun, 1985), p. 11.

66. Wingate, *Tilling the Soul,* pp. 69–71.

67. Krishna, *The Biological Basis.*

68. Saint Teresa, *The Interior Castle,* p. 149.

69. Ibid., p. 179.

70. Saint Catherine of Siena, *The Divine Dialogue of St. Catherine of Siena,* trans. Alger Thorold, 2d ed., (London, 1926).

71. Saint Teresa, *The Interior Castle,* pp. 186, 194.

72. Saint Catherine of Genoa, *Vita Mirabile e Dottrina Celeste di Santa Catherina de Genova,* Insieme Col Trattato del Purgatorio e col Dialogo della Santa, 1743, CAP. XVIII.

73. C. Leadbeater, *The Chakras* (Wheaton, Ill.: the Theosophical Publishing House, 1969).

74. *The Gospel of Thomas,* p. 11.

75. Ibid., Log. 2, p. 10.

76. Einstein, *Ideas and Opinions.*

77. His Divine Grace A. C. Bhaktivedanta Swami Prabhupada, trans., *The Bhagavad-Gita,* with original Sanskrit text and elaborate purports (New York: Collier Books, 1973), pp. 371–7 (7.7–7.12).

78. Robert Ernest Hume, trans., *The Thirteen Principal Upanishads,* from the Sanskrit, with an outline of the philosophy of the Upanishads (London: Oxford University Press, 1971), p. 209.

79. Ibid., p. 31.

80. Ibid., p. 157.

81. Ibid., p. 50.

82. Ibid., p. 43.

83. Ibid., p. 104.

84. Ken Wilber, *Quantum Questions* (London: New Science Library, 1984), p. 27.

85. Bohm, *Wholeness,* p. 174.

86. *The Thirteen Principal Upanishads,* p. 32.

87. Carey, *Vision,* p. 87.

88. Saint Bernard of Clairvaux, *The Steps of Humility* (Cambridge, Ma., 1940).

89. Dhirenda Mohan Datta, *The Philosophy of Mahatma Gandhi* (Madison, Wi.: The University of Wisconsin Press, 1972), p. 30.

90. Bhagavan Das, *The Essential Unity of All Religions* (Wheaton, Ill.: The Theosophical Publishing House, 1973), p. 93.

91. Meher Baba, *Sparks from Meher Baba* (Myrtle Beach, S.C.: Sheriar Press, 1962), pp. 9–10.

92. Das, *The Essential Unity*, p. 98.

93. Ibid., p. 103.

94. Ibid., p. 94.

95. Ibid., p. 110.

96. Ibid.

97. Quoted in Aldous Huxley, *The Perennial Philosophy*, p. 56.

98. Schroedinger, *What Is Life?* p. 88.

99. Das, *The Essential Unity*, p. 60.

100. Swami Rama, *The Book of Wisdom.*

101. Sir James Jeans, *The Mysterious Universe* (Cambridge University Press, 1931), p. 111.

102. Huxley, *The Perennial Philosophy*, p. 14.

103. Meister Eckhart, *Meister Eckhart: A Modern Translation,* trans. R. B. Blankney (New York, 1941).

104. Winkworth, trans., *Theologia Germanica* (London: 1937).

105. Jalaluddin Rumi, *Teachings of Rumi the Masnavi,* trans. and abridged E. H. Whinfield (New York: E. P. Dutton & Co., 1975).

106. Das, *The Essential Unity*, p. 176.

107. Ibid., p. 62.

108. Rabbi Ben Zion Bokser, ed. and trans., *The Essential Writings of Abraham Isaac Kook* (Warwick, N.Y.: Amity House, 1988) p. 167.

109. Freeman J. Dyson, *Infinite In All Directions* (New York: Harper & Row, 1988), pp. 118–9.

110. Swami Prabhupada, *The Bhagavad-Gita,* pp. 371–7.

111. *Cidade Calelixnese* manuscript, found in Oxyrynchus, Egypt, is located in the British Library, Department of Manuscripts, London.

112. Courtney Tower, "Mother Theresa's Work of Grace," in *Reader's Digest,* December 1987, p. 248.

113. Ibid., p. 166.

114. Meher Baba, *God to Man and Man to God,* ed. C. B. Purdom (Myrtle Beach, S.C.: Sheriar Press, Inc., 1975), pp. 23–4.

115. Eckhart, *Meister Eckhart.*

116. Huxley, *The Perennial Philosophy*, p. 22.

117. Julian Huxley, *Aldous Huxley 1894–1963; A Memorial Tribute* (London: Chatto and Windus; New York: Harper & Row), p. 174.

118. Walter M. Abbot and Geoffrey Chapman, eds., *The Documents of Vatican II,* with notes by Protestant and Orthodox authorities, 1966, p. 223.

119. Subramuniya, "Spiritual Unfolding" in *Spiritual Community Guide* (San Rafael: Spiritual Community Publications, 1974), p. 13.

120. Baba, *God to Man,* pp. 16–17.

121. Rumi, Teachings of Rumi, p. 159.

122. *Encyclopedia Britannica* (Chicago: Helen Hemingway Benton, 1975), vol. 15, p. 410.

123. Orest Bedrij, ed., "Union without Ceasing," *Yes, It's Love: Your Life Can Be A Miracle* (New York: Pyramid Publications, 1974), p. 32.

124. Swami Muktananda, *Kundalini,* pp. 47–8.

125. de Chardin, Pierre Teilhard, *The Future of Man* (New York: Harper & Row, 1959).

126. Ibid., pp. 319, 322.

127. Quoted in Tony Rothman, *Discover,* May 1987, p. 96.

128. Sri Aurobindo, *The Light Divine* (New York: the Sri Aurobindo Library, Inc., 1949); idem, *The Future Evolution of Man* (Wheaton, Ill.: The Theosophical Publishing House, 1974).
    C. K. Barrett, *From First Adam to Last: A Study in Pauline Theology* (New York: Scribner, 1962).
    The Bhagavad-Gita in Sanskrit. Many English translations are available, among them that of Swami Prabhavananda and Christopher Isherwood, a Mentor Paperback, 1954; that of Ann Stanford, New York: Herder & Herder, 1971; that of P. Lal, Calcutta: Writers Workshop, 1965; and that of Swami Nikhilanada, New York: Ramakrishna-Vivekananda Center, 1952. Also a complete edition with original Sanskrit text; see note 77.
    Jacob Bochme, *The Incarnation of Jesus Christ,* trans. J. R. Earie (London: Constable, 1934).
    Lucien Cerfaux, Christ in the Theology of St. Paul (New York: Harper & Row, 1959).
    de Chardin, The Future of Man.
    Lecomte DuNouy, *Human Destiny* (New York: Longmans, Green & Co., 1947).
    Allan D. Galloway, *The Cosmic Christ* (New York: Harper Brothers, 1951).
    G. H. C. MacGregor, *St. John's Gospel* (London: Hodder & Stoughton, 1936).
    G. Montague, *Growth in Christ* (Kirkwood, Mo.: Maryhurst Press, 1961).
    L. H. Taylor, *The New Creation* (New York: Pageant Press, 1958). A. Wilkenhause, *Pauline Mysticism* (Freiburg: Herder, 1956).

129. Sheldon Cheney, *Men Who Have Walked with God* (New York: Alfred A. Knopf, 1945), p. 57.

130. Sri Aurobindo, *The Mind Light* (New York: E. P. Dutton & Co., 1953).

131. Swami Rama, *The Book of Wisdom,* p. 109.

132. Maurice R. Bucke, *Cosmic Consciousness: A Study in the Evolution of the Human Mind* (New York: E. P. Dutton & Co., 1901 and 1975).

133. Quoted in Geoffrey Hodson, *The Hidden Wisdom,* p. 42.

134. Maurice Nicoll, *The New Man* (Baltimore: Penguin Books, 1972), p. 20.

135. John C. Haughey, *The Conspiracy of God* (Garden City, N.Y.: Image Books, 1976), p. 24.

136. Milarepa, *One Hundred Thousand Songs,* p. 499.

137. Carey, *Vision,* p. 87.

138. Huxley, *The Perennial Philosophy,* p. 15.

139. Walter J. Burghardt, *The Image of God in Man According to Cyril of Alexandria* (Washington, D.C.: The Catholic University of America, 1957).
    A. Kerrigan, *St. Cyril of Alexandria: Interpreter of the Old Testament* (Rome: 1952).
    John Lawson, *The Biblical Theology of Saint Irenaeus* (London: Epworth Press, 1948).
    J. Lebreton, *History of the Dogma of the Trinity from its Origins to the Council of Nicaea* (London: Burns, Oates, and Washbourne, 1939).
    Emile Mersch, *The Whole Christ* (Milwaukee: Bruce, 1938).
    E. F. Osborne, *The Philosophy of Clement of Alexandria* (Cambridge: Cambridge University Press, 1957).
    R. B. Tollinton, *Clement of Alexandria,* 2 vols. (London: Williams and Norgate, 1914).

140. Quoted in Joseph James, *The Way of Mysticism* (London: Jonathan Cape, 1950), p. 178.

141. Huxley, *The Perennial Philosophy,* p. 12.

142. Ibid., p. 11.

143. Ibid., p. 14.

144. Das, *The Essential Unity,* p. 109.

145. Mechtchild of Magdeburg, *Das Flieszende Licht der Gottheit von Mechtchild von Magdeburg* (*The Flowing Light of the Godhead*) (Berlin, 1909).

146. Gerald Tranter, *The Mystery Teachings and Christianity* (Wheaton, Ill.: The Theosophical Publishing House, 1969), p. 70.

147. Peter Roche de Coppens, *The Nature and the Use of Ritual for Spiritual Attainment* (St. Paul, Minn.: Llewellyn Publications, 1986), p. 73.

148. Huxley, *The Perennial Philosophy.*

149. St. John of the Cross, *The Collected Works of St. John of the Cross,* trans. Kieran Kavanaugh and Otilio Rodriguez (Washington, D.C.: Institute of Carmelite Studies, 1973).

150. His Holiness Pope Paul VI, *Ecclisiam Suam* (New York: Paulist Press, 1965), p. 30.

151. Sri Aurobindo, *Essays on the Gita* (Pondicherry: Sri Aurobindo Ashram Press, 1950); idem, *The Ideal of Human Unity* (New York: Dutton, 1950); idem, *The Life Divine,* vol. 3 of the Sri Aurobindo Center of Education Collection (Pondicherry: Sri Aurobindo Ashram Press, 1960).
    Beatrice Bruteau, *Evolution Toward Divinity: Teilhard de Chardin and the Hindu Traditions* (Wheaton, Ill.: The Theosophical Publishing House, 1974).
    Lao Tzu, *Tao te Ching,* trans. D. C. Lau (Baltimore: Penguin Books, 1963).
    Pantanjali, *How to Know God: The Yoga Aphorisms of Pantanjali,* trans. Swami Praghavanda and Christopher Isherwood (New York: Mentor Books, 1969).
    S. Radhakrishnan, *The Principal Upanishads* (London: Allen & Unwin, 1953).
    Rabindranath Tagore, *The Religion of Man* (London: Allen & Unwin, 1931).
    Pierre Teilhard de Chardin, *Activation of Energy* (New York: Harcourt Brace Jovanovich, 1971); idem, *The Appearance of Man* (New York: Harper & Row, 1956); idem, *Building the Earth* (Wilkes-Barre, Pa.: Dimension Books, 1965); idem, *Christianity and Evolution* (New York: Harcourt Brace Jovanovich, 1971); *The Divine Milieu* (New York: Harper & Row, 1956); idem, *The Future of Man* (New York: Harper & Row, 1964); idem, *Human Energy* (New York: Harcourt Brace Jovanovich, 1960); idem, *Hymn of the Universe* (New York: Harper & Row, 1965); idem, *The Making of a Mind* (New York: Harper & Row, 1956).
    Oliver Reiser, *Cosmic Humanism* (Schenkman, 1966).
    Preston Harold and Winifred Babcock, *Cosmic Humanism and World Unity* (New York: Dodd, Mead, 1971).
    Vedanta Sutras, Sacred Books of the East.

152. Das, *The Essential Unity,* p. 388.

153. Ibid.

154. Dyson, *Infinite in All Directions,* p. 45.

155. Paul Davis, *Superforce* (New York: Simon & Schuster, 1984), p. 5.

156. Alfred North Whitehead, "On Mathematical Method," from *An Introduction to Mathematics* (London: Oxford University Press, 1948).

157. Davis, *Superforce,* pp. 5, 10.

158. E. Amaldi, "The Unity of Physics," in *Physics Today,* September 1973, pp. 23–29.
    Bohm, *Wholeness;* idem, *The Special Theory of Relativity* (New York: W. A. Benjamin, 1965).
    N. Bohr, *Atomic Theory and the Description of Nature* (Cambridge: Cambridge University Press, 1934).
    Max Born, *Atomic Physics* (London: Black & Son Ltd., 1969).

D. A. Bromley, ed., "The Unity of Physics," in *Physics in Perspective* (Washington, D.C.: National Academy of Sciences, 1972), pp. 333–5.

T. E. Clark, T. K. Kuo, N. Nakagawa, "An SO(10) Supersymmetric Grand Unified Theory," Dept. of Physics, Purdue Univ., West Lafayette, Ind., August 1982.

M. Dine, W. Fischler, "A Supersymmetric Gut," Inst. for Advanced Study, Princeton, N.J., *Nucl. Phys. B. Part. Phys.* (Netherlands), vol. B204, no. 3-346-64.20 September 1982.

H. P. Durr, "Radical Unification," Max Planck Inst. Fur Phys. und Astrophys., Munchen, Germany; P. Breitenlohner and H. P. Durr, eds., *Unified Theories of Elementary Particles: Critical Assessment and Prospects.* Proceedings of the Heisenberg Symposium, 36–60, 1982.

Albert Einstein, "Prinzipielles zur Allgemeinen Relativitaetstheorie" (Principles Concerning the General Theory of Relativity), *Ann d. Physik,* 55 (1918), pp. 241–4; idem, "Generalization of Gravitation Theory," a reprint of Appendix II from the fourth edition of *The Meaning of Relativity* (Princeton: Princeton University Press, 1953).

J. Ellis, M. K. Gaillard, D. V. Nanopoulos, Serge Rudaz, "Grand Unification, The Neutron Electric Dipole Moment and Galaxy Formation," Cern, Geneva, Switzerland; *Nature* (GB), vol. 293, no. 5827 41-3, 3–9, September 1981.

J. Ellis, M. K. Gaillard, B. Zumino, "Superunification," Cern, Geneva, Switzerland, ACTA Phys. Pol. B (Poland), vol. B13, no. 4, 253–83, April 1982.

E. Farhi, L. Suskind, "Grand Unified Theory with heavy Color," Stanford Linear Accelerator Center, Stanford Univ., Stanford, Ca., *Phys. Rev. D,* vol. 20, no. 12, 3404–11, 15 December 1979.

R. P. Feynman et al., *The Feynman Lectures on Physics* (Addison-Wesley, 1963–65).

Y. Fujimoto, "SO(18) Unification," International Center for Theoretical Phys., Trieste, Italy, *Phys. Rev. D,* vol. 26, no. 11 318–94, 1 December 1982.

M. K. Gaillard, "Guts, Susy Guts and Super Guts," Dept. of Phys., Univ. of California, Berkeley, Ca., *AIP Conf. Proc.* (USA), no. 93, 291–304, 1982.

H. Georgi, "The Case for and against New Directions in Grand Unification," Lyman Lab. for Phys., Harvard Univ., Cambridge, Ma., USA, M. Konuma; T. Maskawa, eds., *Grand Unified Theories and Related Topics.* Proceedings of the 4th Kyoto Summer Institute 109–41 1981.

John C. Grave, *Conceptual Foundations of Contemporary Relativity Theory* (Cambridge: M.I.T. Press, 1971).

Werner Heisenberg, *Across the Frontiers* (New York: Harper & Row, 1974).

Werner Heisenberg, *Physics and Philosophy* (London: Allen and Unwin, 1958).

W. M. Honig, "Preface to a GUT (Grand Unified Theory)," School of Phys. Sci., Western Australian Inst. of Technol., Perth, Australia, *Speculations Sci. and Technol.* (Switzerland), vol. 5, no. 4, 395–411, October 1982.

J. E. Kim, "Supersymmetric Grand Unification in SO(14)," Dept. of Phys., Seoul Nat. Univ., Seoul, Korea, *Phys. Rev.* D(USA), vol. 26, no. 3 674–90 1 August 1982.

D.V. Nanopoulos, "Tales of the Gut Age," Cern, Geneva, Switzerland; M. Konuma and T. Maskawa, eds., *Grand Unified Theories and Related Topics.* Proceedings of the 4th Kyoto Summer Institute 5-63 1981.

R. E. Peierls, *The Laws of Nature* (George Allen: 1955).

T. G. Rizzo and G. Senjanovic, "Grand Unification and Parity Restoration at Low Energies II," *Unification Constraints,* Brookhaven Nat. Lab., Upton, N.Y., USA, *Phys. Rev. D.* (USA), vol. 25, no. 1, 235–47, 1 January 1982.

M. A. Tonnelat, *Einstein's Unified Field Theory* (New York: Gordon and Breach, Inc., 1966).

Edwin F. Taylor and John A. Wheeler, *Space Time Physics* (San Francisco: W. H. Freeman and Co., 1966).

C. F. von Weizsacker, *The Unity of Physics in Quantum Theory and Beyond,* ed. Ted Bastin (Cambridge: Cambridge University Press, 1971); idem, *The Unity of Nature,* trans. Francis J. Zucker (New York: Farrar, Strauss, Giroux, 1980).

159. David Halliday and Robert Resnick, *Physics for Students of Science and Engineering* (New York: John Wiley & Sons, Inc., 1966), p. 2.

160. Ibid., p. 4.

161. Albert Einstein, in *The New York Post,* November 28, 1972.

162. Rupert Sheldrake, in *Noetic Sciences Review.*

163. Bertrand Russell, *Introduction to Mathematical Philosophy* (New York: The MacMillan Co. and George Allen & Unwin Ltd., 1919), ch. 2.

164. Heisenberg, *The Physicist's Conception of Nature.*

165. Bohm, *Wholeness,* pp. 191-2.

166. Table II equations with equal signs (=) are explained in the books listed below.

Warren B. Boast, *Principles of Electric and Magnetic Fields* (New York: Harper & Brothers, 1950.).

Watson and Montgomery Margenau, *Physics Principles and Applications* (New York: McGraw-Hill Book Co., Inc., 1953).

David Halliday and Robert Resnick, *Physics: Parts I and II* (New York: John Wiley & Sons, 1966).

167. Values, in Table III, have been recommended for general use by the Committee on Data for Science and Technology of the International Council of Scientific Unions (CODATA). The numerical values are given in the International System of Units. (From *Physics Today,* September, 1974).

BIBLIOGRAPHY

Amaldi, E. "The Unity of Physics." *Physics Today.* September 1973.

Athanasius, Saint. *De Incarnatione Verbi.*

Aurobindo, Sri. *Essays on the Gita.* Pondicherry: Sri Aurobindo Ashram Press, 1950. *The Future Evolution of Man.* Wheaton, Ill.: The Theosophical Publishing House, 1974. *The Ideal of Human Unity.* New York: Dutton, 1950. *The Life Divine.* Vol. 3 the Sri Aurobindo Center of Education. Pondicherry: Sri Aurobindo Ashram Press, 1960. *The Light Divine.* New York: The Sri Aurobindo Library, Inc. 1949. *The Mind Light.* New York: E. P. Dutton & Co., 1953.

Baba, Meher. *God to Man and Man to God.* Edited by C. B. Purdom. Myrtle Beach, S.C.: Sheriar Press, 1975. *Sparks from Meher Baba.* Myrtle Beach, S.C.: Sheriar Press, 1962.

Barrett, C. K. *From First Adam to Last, A Study in Pauline Theology.* New York: Scribner, 1962.

Bedrij, Orest, ed. "Union without Ceasing." *Yes, It's Love: Your Life Can Be A Miracle.* New York: Pyramid Publications, 1974.

Bernard of Clairvaux, Saint. *The Steps to Humility.* Cambridge, Ma., 1940.

Bhagavad-Gita, The in Sanskrit. Many English translations are available, among them that of Swami Prabhavananda and Christopher Isherwood, a Mentor Paperback, 1954; that of Ann Stanford, New York: Herder & Herder, 1971; that of P. Lal, Calcutta: Writers Workshop, 1965; and that of Swami Nikhilanada, New York: Ramakrishna-Vivekananda Center, 1952. Also a complete edition with original Sanskrit text by His Divine Grace A. C. Bhaktivedanta.

Swami Prabhupada, New York: Collier Books, 1972.

Boast, Warren B. *Principles of Electric and Magnetic Circuits.* New York: Harper & Brothers, 1950.

Boehme, Jacob. *The Incarnation of Jesus Christ.* Translated by J. R. Earie. London: Constable, 1934.

Bohm, David. *The Special Theory of Relativity.* New York: W. A. Benjamin, 1965. *Wholeness and the Implicate Order.* Boston: Routledge & Kegan Paul Ltd., 1980. Reprint. London: Associated Book Publishers Ltd. (Ark Paperbacks Ltd.), 1983.

Bohr, N. *Atomic Theory and the Description of Nature.* Cambridge: Cambridge University Press, 1934.

Bokser, Ben Zion, Rabbi, ed. and trans. *The Essential Writings of Abraham Isaac Kook* Warwick, N.Y.: Amity House, 1988.

Born, Max. *Atomic Physics* London: Black & Son Ltd., 1969.

Bromley, D. A., ed. "The Unity of Physics." *Physics in Perspective.* Washington, D.C.: National Academy of Sciences, 1972.

Brunton, Paul. *The Hidden Teaching Beyond Yoga* New York: Samuel Weiser, 1972.

Bruteau, Beatrice. *Evolution Toward Divinity: Teilhard de Chardin and the Hindu Traditions.* Wheaton, Ill.: The Theosophical Publishing House, 1974.

Bucke, Maurice R. *Cosmic Consciousness: A Study into Evolution of the Human Mind.* New York: E. P. Dutton & Co., 1901 and 1975.

Burghardt, Walter J. *The Image of God in Man According to Cyril of Alexandria* Washington, D.C.: Catholic University of America, 1957.

Buri, Fritz. *Der Pantokrator, Ontologie und Eschatologie als Grundlage der Lehre von Gott.* Hamburg-Bergstedt: Herbert Reich, 1969.

Carey, Ken. *Vision.* Kansas City, Mo.: Uni Sun, 1985.

Carpenter, Edward. *The Drama of Love and Death.* London: George Allen & Unwin Ltd.

Catherine of Genoa, Saint. *Vita Mirabile e Dottrina Celeste de Santa Catherina de Genova.* Insieme Col Trattato del Purgatorio e col Dialogo della Santa. 1743, CAP. XVIII.

The Divine Dialogue of St. Catherine of Siena. Translated by Alger Thorold. 2d ed. London, 1926.

Cerfaux, Lucien. *Christ in the Theology of St. Paul.* New York: Harper & Row, 1959.

de Chardin, Pierre Teilhard. *The Future of Man.* New York: Harper & Row, 1959. *Activation of Energy,* New York: Harcourt Brace Jovanovich, 1971.

Cheney, Sheldon. *Men Who Have Walked with God.* New York: Alfred A. Knopf, 1945.

Chu Ta-kao, trans. *Tao-te Ching.* Boston, Ma: Mandala Books, 1982.

Cidade Calelixnese manuscript, found in Oxyrynchus, Egypt, is located in the British Library, Department of Manuscripts, London.

Clark, Kenneth. *Civilization: A Personal View.* New York: Harper & Row, 1969.

Clark, T. E., Kuo, T. K., Nakagawa, N. "An SO(10) Supersymmetric Grand Unified Theory." Dept. of Physics, Purdue University, West Lafayette, Ind., August 1982.

de Coppens, Peter Roche. *The Nature and Use of Ritual for Spiritual Attainment* St. Paul, MN: Llewellyn Publications, 1986. *Spiritual Perspective II: The Spiritual Dimension and Implications of Love, Sex and Marriage.* Washington, D.C.: University Press of America, 1981.

Das, Bhagavan. *The Essential Unity of All Religions.* Wheaton, Ill.: The Theosophical Publishing House, Quest Book Edition, 1973.

Datta, Dhirenda Mohan. *The Philosophy of Mahatma Gandhi.* Madison, Wis.: The University of Wisconsin Press, 1972.

Davis, Paul. *Superforce.* New York: Simon & Schuster, 1984.

Descartes, Rene. "Rules for the Direction of the Mind." Translated by Elizabeth S. Haldane and G. R. T. Ross. *The Great Books of the Western World.* Chicago: Encyclopedia Britannica, Inc., 1971, vol. 31.

Dewey, John. *The Influence of Darwin on Philosophy.* New York, 1910.

Dine, M. and Fischler, W. "A Supersymmetric Gut." *Nucl. Phys. B, Part. Phys.,* Institute for Advanced Study, Princeton, N.J. Netherlands. Vol. B204, no. 3-346-64.20, September 1982.

Documents of Vatican II, The, with notes by Protestant and Orthodox authorities. Edited by Walter M. Abbot, Geoffrey Chapman, 1966.

DuNouy, Lecomte, *Human Destiny.* New York: Longmans, Green & Co., 1947.

Durr, H. P. "Radial Unification." Max-Planck Inst. Fur Phys. und Astrophys., Munchen, Germany. Edited by P. Breitenlohner and H. P. Durr. *Unified Theories of Elementary Particles: Critical Assessment and Prospects.* Proceedings of the Heisenberg Symposium 36–60, 1982.

Dyson, Freeman. *Infinite in All Directions.* New York: Harper & Row, 1988.

Eckhart, Meister. *Works* Translated by C. B. Evans. London, 1924.

Einstein, Albert. "Generalization of Gravitation Theory." A reprint of Appendix II from the fourth edition of *The Meaning of Relativity.* Princeton, N.J.: Princeton University Press, 1953. *Ideas and Opinions.* New York: Crown Publishers, 1954. "Prinzipielles zur Allgemeinen Relativitaetstheorie" (Principles Concerning the General Theory of Relativity). *Ann d. Physik,* 55 (1918).

Ellis, J., Gaillard, M. K., Nanopoulos, D. V., Rudas, Serge. "Grand Unification, The Neutron Electric Dipole Moment and Galaxy Formation." Cern, Geneva, Switzerland. *Nature* (GB), Vol. 293, no. 5827 41-3, 3–9, September 1981.

Ellis, J., Gaillard, M. K., Zumino, B. "Superunification." Cern, Geneva, Switzerland. ACTA Phys. Pol. B (Poland) Vol. B13, no. 4 253–83, April, 1982.

d'Estaing, Giscard. *U.S. News and World Report.* March 3, 1975.

Farhi, E., Suskind, L. "Grand Unified Theory with Heavy Color." Stanford Linear Accelerator Center, Stanford University, Stanford, Ca. *Phys. Rev. D*(USA), Vol. 20, no. 12, 3404–11, 15 December, 1979.

Ferguson, Marilyn. *The Brain Revolution.* New York: Taplinger Publishing Company, 1973.

Feynman, R. P. et al. *The Feynman Lectures on Physics.* Addison-Wesley, 1963–65.

Fujimoto, Y. "SO(18) Unification." International Center for Theoretical Phys., Trieste, Italy. *Phys. Rev.* (USA). Vol. 26, no. 11 318–94, 1 December, 1982.

Gaillard, M. K. "Guts, Susy Guts and Super Guts." Dept. of Phys., University of California, Berkeley, Ca. *AIP Conf. Proc.* (USA), No. 93, 291–304, 1982.

Galloway, Allan D. *The Cosmic Christ.* New York: Harper Brothers, 1951.

Georgi, H. "The Case for and against New Directions in Grand Unification." Lyman Lab. for Phys., Harvard University, Cambridge, MA. Edited by M. Konuma and T. Maskawa. *Grand Unified Theories and Related Topics.* Proceedings of the 4th Kyoto Summer Institute 109–41, 1981. *Good News for Modern Man.* New York: American Bible Society, 1970. *Gospel of Thomas, The.* York, England: The Ebor Press, 1987.

Graves, John C. *Conceptual Foundations of Contemporary Relativity Theory.* Cambridge, Ma.: M.I.T. Press, 1971.

Haich, Elizabeth. *Sexual Energy and Yoga.* London: George Allen & Unwin Ltd.

Halliday and Resnick. *Physics for Students of Science and Engineering.* New York: John Wiley & Sons, 1966.

Harold, Preston and Babcock, Winifred. *Cosmic Humanism and World Unity.* New York: Dodd, Mead, 1971.

Haughey, John C. *The Conspiracy of God.* Garden City, N.Y.: Image Books, 1976.

Hawking, W. Stephen. *A Brief History of Time.* New York: Bantam Books, 1988.

Hawkins, Donald, J., ed. *Famous Statements, Speeches and Stories of Abraham Lincoln.* Scarsdale, N.Y.: Heathcote Publications, 1981.

Heisenberg, Werner. *Across the Frontiers.* New York: Harper & Row, 1974. *The Physicist's Conception of Nature.* New York: Harcourt and Brace, 1955. *Physics and Philosophy.* London: Allen and Unwin, 1958.

Hodson, Geoffrey. *The Christ Life from Nativity to Ascension.* London: The Theosophical Publishing House, 1975. *The Hidden Wisdom in the Holy Bible.* (An examination of the idea that the contents of the Bible are partly allegorical.) 3 vols. Wheaton, Ill.: The Theosophical Publishing House, 1955. Lecture Notes from *The School of Wisdom.* Vol. II. Adyar, Madras, India: The Theosophical Publishing House, 1955.

Honig, W. M. "Preface to a GUT (Grand Unified Theory)." School of Physical Science, Western Australian Institute of Technology, Perth, Australia. *Speculations Sci. and Technol.* (Switzerland) Vol 5, no. 4 395–411, October 1982.

Huxley, Aldous. *The Perennial Philosophy.* New York: Meridian Books, 1968.

Huxley, Julian. *Aldous Huxley 1894–1963; A Memorial Tribute.* London: Chatto and Windus; New York: Harper & Row.

Irenaeus, Saint. *Adversus Haereses.* Book V, ch. 28, 4. *The Ante-Nicene Fathers.* Vol. 1. Edited by A. Roberts and J. Donaldson. Grand Rapids, MI: Eerdmans, 1958.

James, Joseph. *The Way to Mysticism.* London: Jonathan Cape, 1950.

James, William. *The Varieties of Religious Experience.* London: Longmans Green, 1919.

Jeans, Sir James. *The Mysterious Universe.* Cambridge: Cambridge University Press, 1931.

John of the Cross, Saint. *The Collected Works of St. John of the Cross.* Translated by Kieran Kavanaugh and Otilio Rodriguez. Washington, D.C.: Institute of Carmelite Studies, 1973.

Kerrigan, A. St. *Cyril of Alexandria: Interpreter of the Old Testament.* Rome, 1952.

Keynes, Geoffrey, ed. *The Writings of William Blake.* London, 1925, 3 vols.

Kim, J. E. "Supersymmetric Grand Unification in SO(14)." Dept. of Phys., Seoul Nat. Univ., Seoul, Korea. *Phys. Rev. D* (USA). Vol. 26, no. 3 674–90, 1 August, 1982.

Krishna, Gopi. *The Awakening of Kundalini.* New York: Dutton, 1975. *The Biological Basis of Religion and Genius.* New York: Harper & Row, 1972. *Higher Consciousness: The Evolutionary Thrust of Kundalini.* New York: The Julian Press, 1974.

Kundalini: The Evolutionary Energy in Man. Berkeley, 1970.

Lao Tzu. *Tao Te Ching.* Translated by D. C. Lau. Baltimore: Penguin Books, 1963.

Lawson, John. *The Biblical Theology of Saint Irenaeus.* London: Epworth Press, 1948.

Leadbeater, C. *The Chakras.* Wheaton, Ill.: The Theosophical Publishing House, 1969.

Lebreton, J. *History of the Dogma of the Trinity from its Origins to the Council of Nicaea.* London: Burns, Oates, and Washbourne, 1939.

MacGregor, G. H. C. *St. John's Gospel.* London: Hodder & Stoughton, 1936.

Mandino, Og. *The Greatest Salesman in the World.* New York: Frederick Fell Publishers, 1973.

Margenau, Watson and Montgomery. *Physics Principles and Applications.* New York: McGraw-Hill Book Company, 1953.

Mechtchild of Magdeburg. *Das Flieszende Licht der Gottheit von Mechtchild von Magdeburg* (The Flowing Light of the Godhead). Berlin, 1909.

Mersch, Emile. *The Whole Christ.* Milwaukee: Bruce & Bruce, 1938.

Merton, Thomas. *The Asian Journal of Thomas Merton.* Edited by Naomi Burton, Brother Patrick Hart, and James Laughlin. New York: New Directions Press, 1973.

Milarepa, Jetsun. *One Hundred Thousand Songs of Milarepa.* Translated and annotated by Garma C. C. Chang. Boulder: Shambala, 1977. 2 vols.

Montague, G. *Growth in Christ.* Kirkwood, Mo.: Maryhurst Press, 1961.

Muktananda, Swami. *Kundalini: The Secret of Life.* South Fallsburg, N.Y.: SYDA Foundation, 1979. *Play of Consciousness.* New York: Harper & Row.

Muller, Robert. *A Planet of Hope.* Warwick, N.Y.: Amity House, 1985.

Nanopoulos, D. V. "Tales of the Gut Age." Cern. Geneva, Switzerland. *Grand Unified Theories and Related Topics.* Edited by M. Konuma and T. Maskawa. Proceedings of the 4th Kyoto Summer Institute 5–63, 1981.

New American Bible, The. Translated from the Original Languages with Critical Use of All the Ancient Sources. Washington, D.C.: Confraternity of Christian Doctrine, 1970.

Nicoll, Maurice. *The New Man.* Baltimore: Penguin Books, 1972.

Origen. *Origenes Werke.* Leipzig, 1899–1925. 8 vols.

Osborne, E. F. *The Philosophy of Clement of Alexandria.* Cambridge: Cambridge University Press, 1957.

Osbourne, Arthur. *Ramana Maharshi and the Path of Self-Knowledge.* New York: Samuel Weiser, 1973.

Pantanjali. *How to Know God: The Yoga Aphorisms of Pantanjali.* Translated by Swami Praghavanda and Christopher Isherwood. New York: Mentor Books, 1969.

Paul VI, His Holiness the Pope. *Ecclesiam Suam.* New York: Paulist Press, 1965.

Peierls, R. E. *The Laws of Nature.* George Allen, 1955.

Planck, Max. *Where Is Science Going?* New York: Norton, 1932.

Plzak, Richard F., Jr. *Paradox East and West.* Unpublished Senior Dissertation, M.I.T., 1973.

Preston, Harold. *Cosmic Humanism and World Unity.* New York: Dodd, Mead, 1971.

Radhakrishnan, S. *The Principal Upanishads.* London: Allen & Unwin, 1953.

Rama, Swami. *The Book of Wisdom.* Kanpur, India: Himalayan International Institute of Yoga, Science & Philosophy, 1972.

Reiser, Oliver. *Cosmic Humanism.* Schenkman, 1966.

Rele, Vasant. *The Mysterious Kundalini.* India: D. B. Taraporevala Sons & Company.

Rizzo, T. G. and Senjanovic, G. "Grand Unification and Parity Restoration at Low Energies II." *Unification Constraints.* Brookhaven Nat. Lab., Upton, N.Y., USA, *Phys. Rev. D.* (USA). Vol. 25, no. 1, 235–47, 1 January, 1982.

Rothman, Tony. *Discover.* May 1987.

Rumi, Jalaluddin. *Teachings of Rumi the Masnavi.* Translated and abridged by E. H. Whinfield. New York: E. P. Dutton & Co., 1975.

Russell, Bertrand. *Introduction to Mathematical Philosophy.* New York: The MacMillan Company and George Allen & Unwin Ltd., 1919.

Sannela, Lee, M.D. *Kundalini—Psychosis or Transcendence?* San Francisco: Sannela, 1976.

Santayana, George. *Reason in Common Sense.* New York: Charles Scribner and Sons, 1927.

Schroedinger, Erwin. *What Is Life?* Cambridge: The MacMillan Company, 1946.

Schure, Edouard. *The Great Initiates.* Translated from the French by Gloria Rasberry. San Francisco: Harper & Row, 1980.

Skolimowski, Henry. "Global Philosophy as the Canvas for Human Unity." *The American Theosophist.* May 1983.

Sky Dancer: The Secret Life and Songs of the Lady Yeshe Tsogyel. Translated by Keith Dowman. London: Routledge & Kegan Paul, 1984.

Subramuniya. "Spiritual Unfolding." *Spiritual Community Guide.* San Rafael: Spiritual Community Publications, 1974.

Tagore, Rabindranath. *The Religion of Man.* London: Allen & Unwin, 1931.

Taylor, Edwin F. and Wheeler, John A. *Space Time Physics.* San Francisco: W. H. Freeman and Co., 1966.

Taylor, L. H. *The New Creation.* New York: Pageant Press, 1958.

Teresa of Avila, Saint. *The Interior Castle.* Translated and edited by E. Allison Peers. Garden City, N.Y.: Image Books, 1944.

The New Encyclopedia Britannica (Chicago: Helen Hemingway Benton, 1973–4) Vol. 2

Theologica Germanica. Translated by Winkworth. London, 1937.

Tollinton, R. B. *Clement of Alexandria.* Vol 1 and 2. London: Williams and Norgate, 1914.

Tonnelat, M. A. *Einstein's Unified Field Theory.* New York: Gordon and Breach, Inc., 1966.

Tower, Courtney. "Mother Theresa's Work of Grace." *Reader's Digest.* December 1987.

Tranter, Gerald. *The Mystery Teachings and Christianity.* Wheaton, Ill.: The Theosophical Publishing House, 1969.

Tzu, Chuang. *Musings of a Chinese Mystic.* London, 1920.

Upanishads, The. Translated from the Sanskrit, with an outline of the philosophy of The Upanishads by Robert Ernest Hume. London: Oxford University Press, 1971.

Vishnu Tirtha, Swami Maharaj. *Devatma Shakti.* India.

Weizsacker, C. F. von. The Unity of Nature. Translated by Francis J. Zucker. New York: Farrar, Strauss, Giroux, 1980. *The Unity of Physics in Quantum Theory and Beyond.* Edited by Ted Bastin. Cambridge: Cambridge University Press, 1971. *The Unity of Nature.* Translated by Francis J. Zucker. New York: Farrar, Strauss, Giroux, 1980.

White, John, ed. *The Highest State of Consciousness.* New York: Doubleday, 1972. *Kundalini, Evolution, and Enlightenment.* New York: Anchor Books/Doubleday, 1978. *Theory and Beyond.* Edited by Ted Bastin. Cambridge: Cambridge University Press, 1971.

Whitehead, Alfred North. "On Mathematical Method." *An Introduction to Mathematics.* London: Oxford University Press, 1984.

Wilber, Ken. *Quantum Questions.* London: New Science Library, 1984.

Wingate. *Tilling the Soul.* Santa Fe, NM: Aurora Press, 1984.

Wilkenhause, A. *Pauline Mysticism.* Freiburg: Herder, 1956.

Zaehner, R. C. *Matter and Spirit: Their Convergence in Eastern Religions, Marx, and Teilhard de Chardin.* New York: Harper & Row, 1963.

Zohar, The. Edited by Soncino. III, 1528, vol. V, p. 211. A good edition of the book of *The Zohar* is that by Christian Knorr von Rosenroth, with Jewish commentaries (Schulzbach, 1684). Reprints with additional index (Amsterdam 1714, 1728, 1722, 1805, 3 vols.). Later editions of *The Zohar* were published at Breslau (1866, 3 vols.); Livorno (1877–78, in 7 parts); and Wilna (1882, 3 vols., 1882–83 in 10 parts); 16, 38.

INDEX

196